# The Dark Side of Cupid:

Love Affairs,
the Supernatural,
and Energy Vampirism

 Keyhole Publishing Company
P.O. Box 92188
Rochester, New York 14692
USA

Copyright ©2012 by Eve Lorgen
All rights reserved. No part of this book may be used or reproduced in any manner whatsoever without written permission except in the case of brief quotations embodied in critical articles or reviews.

Keyhole Publishing Company and logo are
registered trademarks of Keyhole Publishing Company.

Library of Congress Cataloging-in-Publication Data

Lorgen, Evelyn
      The Dark Side of Cupid: Love Affairs, the Supernatural, and Energy Vampirism / by Eve Lorgen
      p. 249
      Includes bibliography.
      ISBN 978-0-9677995-4-4

      I. Lorgen, Eve. II. Title
      Library of Congress Control Number: 2012940303

First published in the United States by Keyhole Publishing Company

First Edition: September 2012

Cover design by Mark Brabant

10  9  8  7  6  5  4  3  2  1

Manufactured in the United States of America.

# The Dark Side of Cupid:
## Love Affairs,
## the Supernatural,
## and Energy Vampirism

## Eve Lorgen

Keyhole Publishing Company

# Contents

Acknowledgments. . . . . . . . . . . . . . . . . . . . . . . . . . . vii

Foreword by Nigel Kerner. . . . . . . . . . . . . . . . . . . . . . . . ix

Introduction. . . . . . . . . . . . . . . . . . . . . . . . . . . . . . . 1

Chapter 1: Why I Wrote This Book. . . . . . . . . . . . . . . . . . . 5

Chapter 2: Who is Cupid?. . . . . . . . . . . . . . . . . . . . . . . 10

Chapter 3: What is The Dark Side of Cupid?. . . . . . . . . . . 22

Chapter 4: The Unholy Triad of the Dark Side of
    Cupid and Questionnaire.. . . . . . . . . . . . . . . . . . . . . 28

Chapter 5: Case Files from The Dark Side of Cupid.
    Category One: Supernatural Influence
    and High Emotional Drama. . . . . . . . . . . . . . . . . . . 33

Chapter 6: Category Two: Mythic Dramas, Spirit
    Guides and Emotional Vampirism. . . . . . . . . . . . . . . 46

Chapter 7: Category Three: Emotional Vampirism
    and Third Party Entities. . . . . . . . . . . . . . . . . . . . . 60

Chapter 8: Category Four: Psychic Vampirism,
    Psychopathic Partners, and Paranormal
    Activity. . . . . . . . . . . . . . . . . . . . . . . . . . . . . . . 77

Chapter 9: Variations on the Dark Side of Cupid:
    Cupid's Interference and Disruption in
    Love Relationships. . . . . . . . . . . . . . . . . . . . . . . 105

Chapter 10: Alien Abduction Cases with Diabolical
    Variations of the Love Bite Theme. . . . . . . . . . . . . 114

Chapter 11: Red Flags. . . . . . . . . . . . . . . . . . . . . . . . . 142

Chapter 12: Vulnerabilities to the
    Dark Side of Cupid.. . . . . . . . . . . . . . . . . . . . . . 152

Chapter 13: Psychological Intervention and
   Communication Strategies.................. 161

Chapter 14: Paranormal Intervention Strategies....... 175

Chapter 15: Grieving the Loss of Your Lover.......... 197

Chapter 16: Is there a Light Side of Cupid?........... 208

Conclusion....................................... 212

Appendix........................................ 216

Suggested Reading............................... 246

About the Author................................ 249

# Acknowledgments

First and foremost, this book is dedicated to my friend and mentor Barbara Bartholic, who passed away in November of 2010. If it hadn't been for Barbara's understanding, support and wisdom, this book would never have been conceived.

My gratitude goes out for all who participated in sharing their stories and anomalous love relationship experiences. Some of them have suffered silently for so many years, and I know how difficult it was for many to even break the silence to become part of this book. My greatest wish is that some day all who have endured such anomalous trauma will not have to be bound by the confines of secrecy and all that entails. Your contributions are greatly appreciated, not only by me but also by those who will benefit from reading about your experiences.

May the light of understanding be freely shared so that our human condition can raise up from its current state into one of true freedom and harmony – especially in love relationships.

# Foreword
by Nigel Kerner

In ancient times the notion that there are powerful yet invisible forces profoundly affecting the lives of individuals was taken as read. Even today there are people from many cultures all over the world who accept these influences as an implicit part of their daily reality. Jinn, dybbuk, succubus, incubus, ghosts, spirits, all these are names from various religions used to describe this same effect.

In the secular western context we are strongly encouraged to believe that all of this is based on superstition and ignorance. Along come the brave knights of Science, riding on their faithful steeds measuring empirically the enforced resolutions of physicality and cutting down with their lances anything they cannot see, hear, smell, taste or touch. Yet most of us are unaware that Science, or 'scientism', the new religion of modern times, is as much faith based as any other religion. As Robert Matthews, science writer, reviewing the latest developments in physics pointed out: "It remains hard to escape the conclusion that there just hasn't been much progress toward answering the Big Questions. That is not to deny that some very significant discoveries have been made and have shown that physicists are far from reaching their summit, and in some cases may be on the wrong path altogether." But Mathews might also admit that all too often these discoveries are subsequently proven suspect or downright wrong. He points out that although key cosmic parameters such as an accurate determination of the age of the universe have been arrived at "put simply, these measurements point to a universe filled with a kind of matter we have never seen and propelled by a force we do not understand. Such a revelation is progress of a sort, but it hardly suggests that the peak of Mount Enlightenment is just over the next hump. The impression is one of physicists not so much approaching a beckoning peak as wandering about in a thick fog." Scientists often raise more questions than they can answer because in measuring with only a partial view, they can see only part of the answer. The more perceptive doyens of science admit this and accept that there is a part that the scientific method can never reach. Perhaps this part is of the most import of all, the part that is the centre of all meaning. After all there is no quark called 'feeling' that they can measure.

As all the great thinkers of the past could testify from Galileo onwards, science ironically progresses out of the premise of being wrong and arguably leaves more casualties in its wake by placing blinkers on the view of its faithful flock and leading them over the precipice than all the wars and conflagrations that have ever happened on the face of the planet.

In Eve Lorgen's remarkable book she explores an aspect of our reality that may well be one of the most powerful driving forces in our world today, the influence on our lives of a non-human intelligence with highly advanced technology at its disposal. Could the demons identified not only by the shamans of traditional societies but also by most of the world's religions in fact be manifestations of extra-terrestrial, or perhaps ultra-terrestrial beings such as this entering uninvited into our sphere of existence and physical reality? If such is indeed the case and unknown to us our lives are to some extent being managed and controlled by entities with an agenda that has nothing to do with our welfare or well being then Eve is doing us a great service in forewarning us of the signs to look out for.

Stephen Hawking and Michio Kaku both believe that not only is it likely that civilizations exist on other planets but also that such civilizations may well be superior to us in technologi-

# Introduction

The Dark Side of Cupid weaves together a trio of significant human passions that are widespread in our culture: true love, the supernatural, and healthy versus toxic relationships. Within the self-help relationship arena alone are universal issues of interest to us all – finding our true love and soul mate, good versus bad relationships and healing from broken hearts. But where, might you ask does the supernatural fit in?

Many of us have experienced something magical or paranormal in our lives at least once, things such as precognitive dreams, omens and synchronicities. A Roper Poll conducted in 1992 on behalf of the Bigelow Holding Company found that 33 million in the U.S. alone have had highly unusual experiences. According to a survey by Jeffrey S. Levin, associate professor at Eastern Virginia Medical School in Norfolk, Virginia, over two-thirds of the U.S. population reported to have had at least one mystical experience. Another survey, conducted in 2006 by researchers from Australia's Monash University, revealed that 70% of the respondents worldwide believed that they had experienced an unexplained paranormal event that changed their life, mostly in a positive way. In addition, 80% believed they had experienced a premonition.

Most paranormal experiences lie in the realm of ghosts, hauntings, vampires, angels, precognition or perhaps even demonic possessions. But rarely, if ever, is any attention placed on the supernatural within the context of human love relationships being orchestrated and interfered with. There are books about love relationships believed to be brought together by divine intervention, mystical tales of how Cupid's arrow magically brought together true soul mates. But it's generally within a positive framework of finding one's true love, twin flame or soul mate. But what about love relationships that have the appearance of being a match made from heaven – but instead end disastrously, as if a supernatural intelligence interlopes as Cupid? A counterfeit soul mate match. Could such a thing happen?

The answer is yes, and this is what I call the Dark Side of Cupid.

For 20 years I have researched and continue to consult with people who experience unusual, emotionally laden traumas. People from all over the U.S. and abroad consult with me in the hope of finding understanding and support regarding their anomalous trauma. In my work, I use the term anomalous trauma to define several types of traumatic experiences, which can include near death experiences, paranormal and UFO related "abduction" events, cults and mind control, and narcissistic abuse. In particular, people who have experienced paranormally influenced, emotionally draining love relationships. This last theme is the focus of this book.

Of all the anomalous experiences under investigation, those that stood out as being extraordinarily traumatic were those that involved love relationships whose onset appeared magical, as if an unseen force had been at work forging powerful psychic connections, only to cascade into a spiral of emotionally draining dramas. Oftentimes, it was the emotionally drained victim of such a love match that came to see me, in hopes of having someone shed insight and to empathize with their story, unbelievable as it may have been. Over the years I've consulted with over fifty individuals who believed their love relationship had been interfered with by unexplained paranormal phenomena or otherworldy entities. I believe there are many more couples that have had paranormal interference, and that my findings only scratch the surface of the magnitude of this unexplained phenomenon.

It is natural human curiosity to try to understand our experience, even if it falls outside the range of what is considered normal. Such experiences can often leave us with emotional scars and anomalous trauma is no different in its effects than other traumatic events in our lives. In fact, anomalous trauma often causes more lasting psychological stress and injury because many who experience these things have had to keep their experiences secret, sometimes for years.

When we experience profound love connections, magical things can happen. Conversely, when we are in a close relationship with a psychologically "toxic" person, we may feel as if an emotional vampire has drained us. On the far end of this spectrum, we may find ourselves with a narcissistic psychopath who seems to have a sixth sense on how to control, manipulate and drain the life out of us.

In *The Dark Side of Cupid*, love relationships, the supernatural and the issue of emotional integrity and psychic vampirism are explored and synthesized together in a coherent way never before done in a self-help book. I examine unusual love relationships in which something magical seemed to happen. But, instead of becoming a delightful and fulfilling soul mate experience, the person was either psychically drained or thrown into an emotionally manipulated, high-drama relationship that had the earmarks of supernatural interference. I leave it to the reader to reflect on who or what the ultimate identity of Cupid really is.

If I had not experienced this myself, or counseled so many others involving these types of love relationships, I would not have believed or even considered such an idea. But now I do.

With this book, I hope to introduce the reader to a new understanding of deeply connected love relationships and apparent soul mates gone wrong. With *The Dark Side of Cupid*, my aim is to challenge the reader to enhance their awareness of the possibility of relationship interference, forged psychic connections and even soul mate counterfeiting. I will also offer tools for recognizing, coping with, healing from and preventing these traumatic, supernaturally influenced love dramas from happening again.

I offer insights, practical skills, healing modalities and renewed hope that a lighter side of Cupid can happen for people. Finding one's soul mate and happiness in love requires emotional maturity and spiritual wisdom. We can retain the magic, wonder and unity of true love, but to do so, we must be discerning.

In my experience, awareness and wisdom had come with a price. This pearl of wisdom I offer to you, in the hope that others do not have to pay such a heavy price of pain and emotional suffering on their journey to find true love. The truth is, what we lack in awareness can and does hurt us. And so, let us be wise in matters of love.

Chapter 1

# Why I Wrote This Book

For twenty years, most of my cases have involved individuals experiencing a moderate degree of paranormal activity, such as a family ghost or demon that affects them, or recurrent events such as alien visitations. Yes, my work largely encompasses alien abductions, encounters, intrusions, whatever one chooses to call them. I believe it's worthy of study and opens a Pandora's Box of questions larger than one can imagine.

It was the many consultations with abductees' unusual love relationships that created my initial theory of the alien love bite. An alien love bite is a sudden infatuation or love obsession with another targeted partner that the aliens – or whoever may be behind this image – appeared to orchestrate between two individuals for a particular type of love drama. I use the term drama because in most cases, the relationship carries severe emotional highs and lows. Sometimes this reaches the point of obsession, leading to emotional trauma and draining of energy for one or both partners. Needless to say, the alien love bite hypothesis is not something easily proven, but it became the name and definition of a type of experience in which its victims felt as if a powerful love match seemed to be set up elsewhere by a supernatural puppet master pulling some very potent emotional strings.

Paranormal activity, emotionally draining dramas, and psychopathic behaviors observed in at least one partner exhibit as major hallmarks of a Dark Side of Cupid love bite. In a later chapter, this is discussed in greater detail as an "Unholy Triad" of symptomatology. At least two of the three indicators are present in all of the cases under study, most manifesting all three parameters, namely: 1) magical/paranormal elements such as omens, precognition and psychic linking, 2) psychic draining, or vampirism, and/or emotional highs and lows, 3) the emotional manipulation and/or psychopathology factor. The deeply connected psychic linking between the two partners often lasts much longer than the love affair itself, and becomes a key feature surrounding the mystery of the Dark Side of Cupid.

The alien love bite theory and the embarrassingly painful effects do not bode well for the popular ufological Disclosure movement, exopolitics theories, and space-brothers-are-here-to-save-us mentality prevalent in the New Age and UFO community. No! Not at all. Nor has it gained acceptance within mainstream psychology circles.

This means that those who experience the trauma of alien abductions and the love bite drama are stranded between a rock and a hard place, isolated in a no man's land where secrecy remains the rule rather than the exception. If disclosure of all things UFO, extraterrestrial, and related secrets ever happens, then the Alien Love Bite and especially the Dark Side of Cupid must be part of this. In my view it may very well be the root driving force behind the ancient extraterrestrial star gods themselves and those powerful clandestine organizations who appear to serve them.

> **If disclosure of all things UFO, extraterrestrial, and related secrets ever happens, then the Alien Love Bite and especially the Dark Side of Cupid must be part of this.**

Some people who contact me keep this part of their lives secret for years, often a decade or more. The alien love bite experience leaves its victims feeling bewildered, emotionally drained, and betrayed not only by their alien visitors (if they know themselves to be abductees), but by the unseen entities that magically arrange the love partnership. It is as if the aliens – or whoever these Cupid interlopers are – leave their victims feeling so profoundly affected that words can barely describe the emotional and psychic pain they must endure. Love bite experiencers are largely disbelieved, even ridiculed, by mainstream media as well as by most psychotherapists and medical professionals. Adding insult to injury, many of their peers within the truth-seeking and disclosure community often ostracize them, as ironic as that sounds.

It has been my observation as an experiencer of alien intrusions, and as a researcher in the fields of alien abduction and anomalous trauma, that ostracism and criticism are inevitable consequences of telling the truth about one's experiences. This happens in mainstream circles as well as the truth-seeking community. There is peer pressure in the New Age community to perceive alien visitations in a certain way. The popular "flavor of the week" (channeled entities, ego-swelling "starseed specialness", high drama, prophetic predictions) tends to get media attention. Left out are usually those individuals who refuse to cater to peer pressure to promote certain New Age agendas. This happened to one of the abductees presented in the case histories in this book, whose experience is highlighted in greater detail in the Appendix. This is one example only, but many others who have come to me with their issues related to the love bite were rejected by other well-known researchers. In fact, many who formerly believed in their aliens as friends or channelled ET entities as benefactors, were assailed with reprisals and spiritual warfare when these entities were seriously challenged. Often a "love bite" orchestrated relationship was the result of such a challenge, where the person dared to question the almighty ET, channelled entity, alien handler or popular viewpoints.

As a counselor, I know that when we face reality-shattering traumatic experiences, we often go into denial, or at least try to minimize the most painful and outlandish aspects of the experience. However, secrecy exacerbates the trauma, and keeps it locked within a freeze frame compartment. It's like living in an emotional concentration camp. I know, because I've had to live it, and would not wish this pain upon my worst enemy.

I admit that my motivation to research this subject originated from my own experiences while growing up in the San Francisco Bay Area, and later while living in Southern California. Several family members and I had UFO sightings as well as sporadic incidents of paranormal activity. In fact, the paranormal activity increased as I researched alien abductions and related phenomena.

It was the mentorship of the late researcher and hypnotherapist Barbara Bartholic who opened my eyes to the dark underbelly of her discoveries while working with alien abductees for over thirty years. Barbara's and my own first hand observations of the devastating and unbelievable effects of alien abduction, interference with human emotions, spirituality, and especially love obsessions, are enough to shock one's senses. In truth, this work has only begun.

Barbara and I discussed alien abduction cases for years, but we tended to talk more about the widespread aspects of how the aliens – perhaps Cupid's Interlopers – matched people together in endless dramas, for example, love obsessions that leave one person emotionally devastated and pining away in unrequited love.

After counseling alien abductees and experiencers for decades, we noticed how various alien species interact and play humanity like one big "Nintendo Game," as Barbara put it. The issue is really much larger than the alien abductee and paranormal experiencer subpopulation. In fact, only 60% of those who reported a Dark Side of Cupid love relationship in this book believed themselves to be "experiencers" of alien visitation.

The Dark Side of Cupid is not exclusive to alien-extraterrestrial interference, but something much deeper, and yet the alien factor cannot be denied either for those who strongly believed themselves to have had alien abductions. These paranormal experiencers become the lens through which we see something much larger going on today – and perhaps having gone on for millennia. Cupid is alive and well. Emotional drama fascinates and feeds him.

# Chapter 2

# Who is Cupid?

For most of us, Cupid is the Roman god of erotic love. He equates with the Greek god Eros. His name, from the Latin word *cupido*, translates into passion, desire, yearning, wanting, or longing. In Latin, Cupid is known as *amor*, which means love, infatuation, or passion. Today, Cupid usually appears as a cherubic angel-fairy who spreads love and romance. The popular image depicts him as a nude young boy, armed with a bow and a quiver of arrows.

However, in ancient times Cupid could be fickle and even perverse. He was, in fact, a bad boy. He often appeared with two sets of arrows, one set made of gold, the other of lead. Although the golden arrows inspired true love, the lead arrows inspired lust or even hatred. Yes, couples could be inspired to hatred from his arrows. Even when causing unsuspecting men and women to fall madly in love, Cupid's motives were not necessarily for their benefit. Rather, he sought to drive them crazy with intense passion, to make their lives miserable, and to laugh at the results.

There is debate as to Cupid's real origin and lineage. In *Theogony*, the ancient Greek poet Hesiod wrote that Cupid, as Eros, was created by two gods, Chaos and the Earth, working together. In these ancient myths, Eros was represented as a full-grown and very beautiful youth, crowned with flowers and leaning on a shepherd's hook.*

Over the course of time, the beautiful and benevolent image faded away, and Cupid became the son of Venus or

---

* The ancient Hindu myths also depicted a Cupid figure, known as Kamadeva, the God of love and sexuality. Some have inferred that this form can also associate with Krishna, an archetype of the divine child.

Aphrodite. It was here that his character developed a mischief-loving side, both good and evil. In yet other tales, he was the son of Venus and Mars, and Nyx and Erubus, the latter of which suggests his more perverse evil-twin lineage.

Whatever the true character of Cupid, his most charming myth is the story known as Eros and Psyche. It originates as a story told by an old woman in Lucius Apuleius' work, *The Golden Ass*, written in the second century A.D. One understands this story best as an allegory, where an ancient archetype of gods and humans springs to life in a drama, displaying important teachings. It is also important to understand that the Greek word *psyche* means, spirit, breath, life, or animating force. In Greek mythology, Psyche is the deification of the human soul, often portrayed as a goddess with butterfly wings.

A shortened version of the myth follows:[*]

> Envious and jealous of the beauty of a mortal girl named Psyche, Venus asks her son, Cupid, to use his golden arrows while Psyche sleeps, so that when she awakens, Venus would have already placed a vile creature for her to fall in love with. Cupid finally agrees to her commands after a long (and failed) debate. As he flies to Psyche's room at night, he turns himself invisible so no one can see him fly in through her window. He takes pity on her, for she was born too beautiful for her own safety. As he slowly approaches, careful not to make a sound, he readies one of his golden arrows. He leans over Psyche while she is asleep and before he can scratch her shoulder with the arrow, she awakens, startling him, for she looks right into his eyes, despite his invisibility. This causes him to scratch himself with his arrow, falling deeply in love with her. He cannot continue his mission, for every passing second he finds her more appealing. He

---

[*] From Wikipedia: http://en.wikipedia.org/wiki/Cupid_and_Psyche

reports back to Venus shortly after and the news enrages her.

Venus places a curse on Psyche that keeps her from meeting a suitable husband, or any husband at that. As she does this, it upsets Cupid greatly, and he decides as long as the curse stays on Psyche, he will no longer shoot arrows, which will cause Venus's temple to fall.

Venus punshes Eros, by Agostino_Carracci [Wiki Commons]

After months of no one – man or animal – falling in love, marrying, or mating, the Earth starts to grow old, which causes concern to Venus, for nobody praises her for Cupid's actions. Finally, she agrees to listen to Cupid's demands, according him one thing to have his own way. Cupid desires Psyche. Venus, upset, agrees to his demands only if he begins work immediately. He accepts the offer and takes off, shooting his golden arrows as fast as he can, restoring everything to the way it should be. People again fall in love and marry, animals far and wide mate, and the Earth begins to look young once again.

When all continue to admire and praise Psyche's beauty, but none desire her as a wife, Psyche's parents consult an oracle, which tells them to leave Psyche on the nearest mountain, for her beauty is so great that she is not meant for (mortal) man. Terrified, they have no choice but to follow the oracle's instructions. But then Zephyrus, the west wind, carries Psyche away, to a fair valley and a magnificent palace where she is attended by invisible servants until nightfall; and in the darkness of night the promised bridegroom arrives and the marriage is consummated. Cupid visits her every night to sleep with her, but demands that she never light any lamps, since he does not want her to know who he is until the time is right.

Cupid allows Zephyrus to take Psyche back to her sisters and bring all three down to the palace during the day, but warns that Psyche should not listen to any argument that she should try to discover his true form. The two jealous sisters tell Psyche, then pregnant with Cupid's child, that rumor is that she had married a great and terrible serpent who would devour her and her unborn child when the time came for it to be fed. They urge Psyche to conceal a knife and oil lamp in the bedchamber, to wait till her husband is asleep, and then to light the lamp and slay him at once if it is as they said. Psyche sadly follows their advice. In the light of the lamp Psyche recognizes the fair form on the bed as the god Cupid himself. However, she accidentally pricks herself with one of his arrows, and is consumed with desire for her husband. She begins to kiss him, but as she does, a drop of oil falls from her lamp onto Cupid's shoulder and wakes him. He flies away, and she falls from the window to the ground, sick at heart.

Psyche then finds herself in the city where one of her jealous elder sisters lives. She tells her what had happened, and then tricks her sister into believing that Cupid has chosen her as a wife on the mountaintop. Psyche later meets her other sister and deceives her as well. Each sister goes to the top of the peak and jumps down eagerly, but Zephyrus does not bear them and they fall to their deaths at the base of the mountain.

Psyche searches far and wide for her lover, finally stumbling into a temple where everything is in slovenly disarray. As Psyche is sorting and clearing the mess, Ceres (Demeter to the Greeks) appears, but refuses any help beyond advising Psyche that she must call directly on Venus, who caused all the problems in the first place. Psyche next calls on Juno in her temple, but Juno gives her the same advice. So Psyche finds a temple to Venus and enters it. Venus then orders Psyche to separate all the grains in a large basket of mixed kinds before nightfall. An ant takes pity on Psyche, and with its ant companions, separates the grains for her.

Venus is outraged at her success and tells her to go to a field where golden sheep graze and to retrieve some golden wool. A river-god tells Psyche that the sheep are vicious and strong and will kill her, but if she waits until noontime, the sheep will go to the shade on the other side of the field and sleep; she can then pick the wool that sticks to the branches and bark of the trees. Venus next asks for water flowing from a cleft that is impossible for a mortal to attain and is also guarded by great serpents. This time an eagle performs the task for Psyche.

Venus, furious at Psyche's survival, claims that the stress of caring for her son, made depressed and ill as a result of Psyche's lack of faith, has caused her to lose some of her beauty. Psyche is to go to the Underworld and ask the queen of the Underworld, Proserpina, to place a bit of her beauty in a box that Venus had given to Psyche. Psyche decides that the quickest way to the Underworld is to throw herself off some high place and die, and so she climbs to the top of a tower. But the tower itself speaks to Psyche and tells her the route that will allow her to enter the Underworld alive and return again, as well as telling her how to get past Cerberus (by giving the three-headed dog a small cake); how to avoid other dangers on the way there and back; and most importantly, to eat nothing but coarse bread in the underworld, as eating anything else would trap her there forever. Psyche follows the orders precisely, rejecting all but bread while beneath the Earth.

However, once Psyche has left the Underworld, she decides to open the box and take a little bit of the beauty for herself. Inside, she can see no beauty; instead an infernal sleep arises from the box and overcomes her. Cupid (Eros), who had forgiven Psyche, flies to her, wipes the sleep from her face, puts it back in the box, and sends her back on her way. Then Cupid flies to Mount Olympus and begs Jupiter (Zeus) to aid them. Jupiter calls a full and formal council of the gods and declares that it is his will that Cupid marry Psyche. Jupiter then has Psyche fetched to Mount Olympus, and gives her a drink made from ambrosia, granting her immortality. Begrudgingly, Venus and Psyche forgive each other.

What can we learn from this myth?
One thing that immediately strikes me as suspect in this

myth is the gods' jealousy of Psyche's beauty. Also, as I mentioned earlier, the Greek word *psyche* means soul. This has a symbolic message in that Cupid, as one of the gods, fell in love with the human soul – the human soul being a feminine archetypal aspect.

The gods harbor both love and jealousy for the human soul. Why? This leads me to question whether we, as humans having immortal souls, are vastly different from these gods. Do we have something that they lack – that they want?

I also have to wonder if Cupid, perhaps with an ability to dream walk interdimensionally, is having blissful astral sex with Psyche? Could he be a shapeshifter and actually have another true form? The invisible lover tells her she cannot see his true form until the time is right. So the chosen beauty, meant for no mortal man, must keep this a secret for now. And who decides when the time is right? The myth never lets us know this. Secrecy rules here.

Cupid allows Psyche to visit her sisters in the earth world, but warns her not to listen to their arguments to discover his true form. I wondered, *why*? Could they be accurate? In fact, Psyche's sisters do try to convince Psyche – albeit out of jealousy – that her lover must be a terrible serpent. The sisters goad Psyche to slay her husband before he kills her. So, in the dark of night, she intends to slay Cupid; however, she recognizes his beautiful form as the God himself. Cupid, being discovered, is hurt and flees because of Psyche's suspicion, doubt, and lack of faith.

Psyche searches far and wide for her long lost lover, encountering various allies and tests along the way. It appears she is being punished for her curiosity and lack of faith. She cannot be reunited with Cupid until she passes each test, which is made almost impossible by Venus's jealous, punishing behaviors. With each test, something synchronistically happens to aid Psyche at the last moment. Even with the impossible nature of the situation, it appears that divine providence is on Psyche's side to enable her to join her true love.

While she is in the Underworld, her curiosity compels her once again to open a box that contains beauty. But, instead of finding beauty, a dark sleep overcomes her. Obviously, she is being tested to follow instructions. So, is this familiar theme – curiosity or knowledge being punished by darkness and lack of awareness – a kind of fall from grace? Would continued curiosity open her eyes to Cupid's true nature, perhaps even to her own?

At this point Cupid forgives Psyche and awakens her, and they return to Mount Olympus, begging the God Zeus to help them. At this point we might wonder, why beg for true love? To beg is to take a stance of powerlessness, vulnerability, and dependence upon an external source, rather than our own innate, divine resources. Again and again, throughout the ages, humanity has set itself up, waiting for rescue from some savior, whether this be a pantheon of gods, a single deity, or extraterrestrials. I question this savior myth. It sets us up to be slaves.

> **This leads me to question whether we, as humans having immortal souls, are vastly different from these gods. Do we have something that they lack – that they want?**

What is wrong with curiosity that leads to expanded awareness and self-responsibility, so that we can make our own choices? What is wrong with a knowledge of good and evil? My question is whether these gods – Venus, Cupid, and the entire pantheon – are working as middlemen, so to speak, to co-opt true divinity so that we fail to realize the depth of our own inner resources. And through our lack of awareness, they milk us in the process in endless dramas and unrequited love affairs. Some of these connections appear to be blissful arrangements by Cupid, but others are full of strife and unrequited love. This is clearly demonstrated in the alien love bite scenarios I have written about previously, and also with the Dark Side of Cupid love connections – as we will see in the case histories that follow.

Do we really need these "saviors," or is it the other way around? In my view, many ETs and aliens are doing the same thing. Perhaps they are co-opting this myth, or perhaps they are the original entities behind the pantheon of gods in our ancient myths.

The Cupid-Psyche myth ends as the council of gods convenes. There, Psyche is allowed the ambrosia of immortality, so that she and Cupid can live happily ever after. Through this sacred marriage, Venus and Psyche also forgive one another.

Since Psyche represents the human soul, this mythical allegory signifies that the soul, before it can be reunited to its original divine Beloved, must be purified by the chastening sorrows and sufferings of its earthly life.

And yet, one must ask whether this myth has been co-opted by another type of God – a darker Cupid?

What Would a Dark Cupid Look Like?

If the good Cupid is depicted as a beautiful winged angel, yet invisible to our normal levels of perception, what would a dark Cupid look like? How might he behave?

Recall that Psyche's sisters warned her that Cupid might be a serpent. We might wonder why they would be afraid of this possibility. What did they know during this mythical time of serpents that could shapeshift and carry off beautiful women for their own pleasure?

Again, we must ask if there is something about the human soul that is irresistible to these ancient mythical gods. Do we have something that they lack, perhaps an immortal soul? Are these gods nothing more than false gods?

Perhaps this is the secret that the Dark Cupid doesn't want us to know.

I have wondered if there is some truth to the Cupid myth, and especially the power of archetypes. By archetype I mean images, symbols or innate prototypes of ideas, which manifest as psychological types or even complexes.* An archetype is like a psychological instinct or informational field of influence, which patterns our psyche, our experience of the world around us, and how we experience ourselves.

The four best-known types of archetypes defined by the pioneer psychologist Carl Jung are: the self, the shadow, the anima, and the animus. Many of us may know them as Greek dieties, or as even more ancient motifs such as the lover, the divine child, the maiden, mother or crone, trickster, warrior, dreamer, hero and so forth. Archetypes act as powerful living energies of the collective unconscious that affect all human beings. They are also the bridge between the realms of logic and intuition.

When archetypes are invoked, synchronicities manifest. Synchronicities are often described as meaningful coincidences, which evoke in us the feeling that we are not alone, that there is a silent observer that shares our lives, and who dreams with us. It is as if the events in our lives are orchestrated by a supernatural source. This is a personal observation, as well as by many mystics, lucid dreamers, artists, and lovers. When one taps into these subconscious archetypal levels of being, deep shifts can occur in our consciousness and our reality. Perhaps this is a result of immersing ourselves into a deeper pool of connectedness with our Beloved and with the collective consciousness in general. Powers of manifestation emerge when we connect more fully with a universal beingness and go with a flow of unity.

---

* http://www.new-age-spirituality.com/philos/jung.html

Synchronicities occur when we step out of the personal dimension of our experience and access what is called the archetypal dimension of experience. I believe this can happen when two people are in love. It also can happen when one has an expanded consciousness that delves beyond the personal and limiting ego boundaries. When this happens, we may also find ourselves playing roles in mythic and divine dramas. Creativity is unleashed when we access this deeper part of ourselves.

It is as if there is a superconscious factor deep within us, arranging our experiences so as to help us awaken. Could we experience this as something that comes from gods outside of us, testing us until we realize our true nature? Perhaps this is why these gods continually interact with humanity.

Jung said that an individuated person would actually shape events around himself or herself through the communication of that person's consciousness with the collective unconscious. He spoke of synchronicity as being an "acausal connecting principle" (i.e., a pattern of connection that is not explained by causality).

In my case studies, meaningful coincidences occur once the Cupid archetype is awakened. Perhaps subconscious desires of love catalyze the train of synchronicities, but whatever transpires, it has the feel of a powerful and unusual happening. These are not simple love affairs gone wrong.

In so many of the love bite cases I have investigated, the lovers enter a magical world where unusual situations unfold with synchronicities and omens. When we are in love, we can access a deeper power within ourselves, which I believe sometimes includes psychic abilities. Perhaps in this sense, Cupid acts as a catalyst of our own creative power. But with the Dark Side of Cupid, instead of a happily-ever-after lesson, the love affair left one of the lovers confused and emotionally drained. For some, it shattered their illusions of love and romance. However, for a rare few, this experience, though painful, woke them up to a greater awareness of reality itself.

In the Dark Side of Cupid, perhaps we have new lessons to be learned, and new myths about love and romance to create and realize. But first, we must recognize what is happening, cope with it, and heal from the emotional trauma and confusion.

Chapter 3

# What is The Dark Side of Cupid?

This chapter describes the basic characteristics of love dramas that appear magically arranged, and yet leave one or both partners feeling emotionally depleted, bewildered, and questioning whether Cupid exists.

When it comes to love, logic can escape us. Momentarily at least, we fall into a magical realm full of infinite possibilities, where we can cast aside our logical selves and embrace the unknown mysteries of love. At last, perhaps we find "the one," our soul mate, our twin flame.

Each person in love may have one particular reason to believe that their new love is true love. Telltale signs appear that he or she must be "the one." A powerful, mystical connection seems to catalyze the love affair's unfolding. It's not simply the physical attraction, but something much more, an unseen quality or series of events that thrust the would-be lovers together, as if directed by Cupid himself – or perhaps his interloper.

No, I'm not talking about traditional arranged marriages, or incidents where a person knowingly casts a magical love spell on a desired lover.* I'm talking about otherwise ordinary people from all walks of life, professions, intelligence, and cultures who experience extraordinary circumstances manifesting as matches made from heaven, in which unusual aspects of a love relationship unfold. These are people who experience supernatural overtones, sometimes for the first time, within the context of a love relationship. Whether in the

---

* Although in a later chapter one such case describes a love connection that is believed to be a result of genuine magic.

form of precognitive hunches, powerful dreams, *déjà vu*, synchronicities or a feeling that the match was a drama manipulated by an invisible force, all were left feeling confused and emotionally drained.

In my caseload of anomalous love relationships, I set out to find the main factors associated with the Dark Side of Cupid. Over a span of twenty years, I've counseled victims of various types of trauma and abuse, those in recovery from addictions, and people involved in anomalous trauma and the paranormal. Anomalous trauma can be anything from supernatural experiences, near death accounts, mind control, cult abuse, alien abductions, time travel reality shifts, or even shamanic initiations.

I've studied countless relationship self-help books dealing with toxic relationships, trauma and addictions, emotional vampires, dangerous men, and psychopathology. And yet none of these books ever recognize or mention anything near to what I am seeing. None address the paranormal element of orchestration and interference in conjunction with being drained

> **Telltale signs appear that he or she must be "the one." A powerful, mystical connection seems to catalyze the love affair's unfolding. It's not simply the physical attraction, but something much more.**

emotionally, in a powerfully connected love relationship that doesn't end well. While there is often a level of psychopathology present in one of the partners, such as addiction or narcissism, it does not explain other anomalous characteristics of the relationship.

Psychic and emotional vampirism is a key feature, and yet

the vampirism itself may be an indirect aspect of the relationship interference — as opposed to being the sole fault of one partner, a.k.a. the energy vampire. In other words, the emotionally draining effects of the relationship may be a result of one partner who acts as a portal or some sort of conduit for another entity, such as Dark Cupid. This Dark Cupid's job is to hijack the energetic component of the love relationship. In other words, the greater the emotional drama, the more energy for Cupid to feed upon.

I believe there are a growing number of cases where something new is emerging that does not fit the standard mental health descriptions and typical psychodynamics of love relationships.

The people involved in the unusual love relationships described in this book are mostly experiencers of the paranormal. They tend to be highly perceptive, sensitive people. Nevertheless, as my research and consulting continue, I also hear from clients who don't have much interest in the paranormal, nor have any evident anomalous trauma in their backgrounds. These are everyday people who seem to be hit over the head with a powerful love match that leaves them barely able to cope. It also leaves them questioning their worldview. Because at some point, their long-held beliefs about reality are seriously challenged.

*Are you on the Dark Side of Cupid's Hit List? When it feels like a match made in heaven.*

The meeting could be accidental, in an unusual place or situation for you. But somehow, something magically happens that creates an opportunity. Perhaps you feel a premonition, energetic feelings that seem to happen out of the blue. Then your eyes meet.

There is a sense of familiarity, as if you already know this strange new person, perhaps from another place or time. Yet, you can't seem to place it. The locked gaze, the sensation of butterflies swirling in your stomach, the feeling of excitement, anxiety, and perhaps even danger all lurk inside you. You can barely contain the sense that something big is happening.

Maybe he or she asks you something that was on your mind, just as you were going to speak it. "Have we met before? You seem familiar." A few moments pass, and maybe you experience a feeling of *déjà vu*. Perhaps you recall a recent dream when you saw the face of your could-be lover. He or she is wearing the same color that appeared in your dream, or perhaps appears in a familiar scene. You now feel that the dream was some sort of divine precognitive foreshadowing. Your dream lover has come to life.

Your senses feel heightened, more alive. Those zingy, tingly, warm, and fuzzy feelings in your body seem to be resonating with this other person. Did you just meet The One? Your soul mate? Is this a sign that person is about to enter center stage in your life?

You exchange phone numbers and email. Next time you meet, you talk about things that you thought no one would ever really share with you, much less understand. You seem to have so much in common. Perhaps the person is not normally your type, yet inexplicably you share a powerful connection. The erotic fantasies begin. Somehow they feel so much more real. Why is that?

From deep inside, however, you feel a subtle hint of push-pull resistance. Your inner voice tries to check in with you, but you squash it like a bug. Your logical mind may question all this, especially if you or the other person already has a partner or spouse. It's taboo and you don't want to flirt with the possibility of infidelity. But the lonely part of you can't stop wanting excitement, a rescue from that hopeless feeling that you'll never have true love and will always settle for less. You want to experience passion and love that you've never really known before. You fight both sides of yourself as if you've been split into two people. Confusion sets in, and you just can't stop thinking about that person.

*The Love Connection Begins and Cupid's Drama Unfolds*

A series of magical phone calls, texting, emailing, and meetings begin. Perhaps you are compelled to drive long distances or even go across the country to meet with your newfound lover-to-be. The energies of excitement build, and you can't stop thinking about him or her, and especially about when you can have more time together to really connect, touch. Merge.

You never felt such a powerful connection with someone; it's almost telepathic with supernatural overtones. You finish each other's sentences, buy similar things at the store, find yourself wearing the same colors, and even eating the same food when not in each others' presence, and at the same times.

That first kiss sends electrical thrills that zip right down to your erogenous zones. It's almost like you've been zapped by Cupid's arrow! You kiss again, deeply. It happens so easily, so fast. Sex feels so natural and connected. You find yourself doing things you didn't do with other partners. You feel less inhibited and the creative juices flow. You take greater risks that may be out of character for you. You push away confusion and the inner red-flag voice flailing to be heard because, you say to yourself, *"Yes! I'm going to follow my heart. I want passion!"*

Now the roller coaster drama begins, and your life turns upside down. He or she makes you feel on top of the world, desired, cherished, and important. Events seem magically to unfold as though a divine script were being written that has pierced through the wall of your lonely heart. You are on a blissful high.

Yet, it doesn't last. Something happens.

At some point, where you once felt excitement and passion, you wonder why you begin to feel weak and a little drained. Maybe your partner reveals a dark side. Emotional manipula-

*Chapter 3: What is the Dark Side of Cupid?*

tion starts to unveil. Is your partner deliberately manipulating you like an emotional vampire, or does it just seem like it? You don't want to believe it. The emotional crashing lows begin, and you start to feel that events are unfolding out of your control. Your partner's full attention and presence seem to be out of your reach, and your life becomes an endless chase of unconsummated love.

Eventually, unrequited love pangs tear at your heart as you and your lover are buffeted about in one drama after another. In time, you become an emotional wreck. Confusion sets in and it seems as though every time you get near Cupid's lover, you become weaker. You feel sucked dry of your emotions, logic, and better sense.

What happened?

Chapter 4

# The Unholy Triad of the Dark Side of Cupid and Questionnaire

After two decades of researching and counseling victims of unusual love relationships, I have identified three main characteristics of the Dark Side of Cupid. When two of these characteristics are present, I consider that we are dealing with an arrow from the Dark Side of Cupid.

*Category #1: The Magical or Supernatural Element*

Magical and supernatural elements happen right before or during the love affair. Synchronicities, omens, precognitive dreams, spirit visitations, insights, vivid dreams, feelings of *déjà vu,* and other paranormal activity may occur. The love match seems to be influenced from The Beyond, as if it were meant to be. Whether or not this can be proven to be true, that is how it feels to at least one of the lovers. This paranormal component is independent of psychopathology or delusion, and is not part of any mental illness. It is important to emphasize that the supernatural qualities alone do not denote a dark matched love relationship.

*Category #2: Emotional Highs and Lows, and/or Emotional Draining*

Emotional highs and crashing lows start to transpire as the love infatuation or obsession unfolds. Emotional draining manifests and could lead to physical exhaustion and confusion. You could be perceived as being on a pedestal with ecstatic feelings and ego boosting episodes, then suddenly let down to an emotional low, either by the partner or through events out of your control. Lots of drama takes place, where tension is key to throwing you off balance. A series of coincidences may occur which creates an unending feeling of unconsummated love, or a wild goose chase to get your lover's attention, but it's never enough to satisfy your yearnings. Unrequited love may set in. This basic trend can be understood as a form of emotional or psychic vampirism depending on its severity and paranormal manifestations.

*Category #3: Emotional Manipulation and the Psychopathology Element*

You or your partner have unusually controlling, manipulative, abusive or attention-getting behaviors, such as psychopathic narcissism or a Jekyll-Hyde duality. You or your partner may also exhibit a paranormal controlling influence suggestive of demonic overshadowing or possession. Perhaps one of you channels a particular spirit guide, ET, or entity that gradually takes over one's personality and then the relationship itself. This can happen in cult groups, and cult leaders particularly fit this psychopathic profile.

*Vulnerability Factors*

When questioning individuals about these situations, in addition to the unholy triad of characteristics listed above, I also look for factors that indicate heightened vulnerability either before or during the time of the love match-drama. I seek realistic patterns which may indicate vulnerability to being targeted by a psychopathological partner, or by unseen paranormal influences. These patterns may include someone who is:

1) Financially and/or economically compromised.
2) Financially well off or recently came into a lot of money or assets.
3) Attracted to powerful people such as in the entertainment industry, music, religious gurus or icons, or powerful people magnets.
4) Involved in a healing profession such as social work,

counseling, nursing, psychic intuitive work, teaching, and the giving, caretaking and nurturing professions.
5) Involved in research into the paranormal, spirituality, conspiracy, and alternative media.
6) Shy, soft spoken, or lacking assertiveness.

In addition to the vulnerability factors, I ask personal questions which elicit a deeper understanding of the magical and supernatural elements, as well as other factors of the triad of the Dark Side of Cupid. I ask questions that mainstream therapists may not consider in their clinical work, but which I find relevant as a researcher of Anomalous Trauma. Here I try to get a better understanding if the love match holds a greater tendency to any one of the factors, namely, (1) the sense of the relationship having been magically arranged from elsewhere, (2) the emotionally draining, unconsummated love drama, and (3) the psychopathology element.

This is the basic Dark Side of Cupid questionnaire that I ask my clients to fill out:

*Do these main characteristics seem familiar to you?*

1. Magical and Supernatural elements that preceded or occurred during the love affair. Things such as synchronicities, precognitive dreams, insights, vivid dreams and feelings of deja vu. Paranormal activity. Love match seems to have been influenced from the beyond, as if it was meant to be. A very strong connection with the person. Y/N
2. Emotional highs and crashing lows, emotional and psychic draining. You may have been perceived on a pedestal with ecstatic feelings, then were suddenly let down to an emotional low, either by the partner or through events out of your control. Lots of drama. Y/N
3. Emotional Manipulation and the Psychopathology Element. Did your partner have unusually controlling, manipulative or abusive and attention-getting behaviors such as:

    a) Histrionic, drama king/queen, endless talking, chatter,

*Chapter 4: The Unholy Triad*

      attention seeker Y/N

  b) Addictive and compulsive, drugs, alcohol, sex, work, sports Y/N

  c) Controlling, jealous, emotional manipulator, passive aggressive Y/N

  d) Narcissistic, lack of empathy, exaggerated sense of entitlement, praise seeking, needs constant attention and superiority complex Y/N

  e) Passive, "yes-but" whiner-victim, very needy Y/N

  f) Extreme narcissist, or Dr. Jekyll/Mr. Hyde duality, bordering on demonic possession or hosting. Supernatural qualities, like black magic, hypnotic control of victim as if you are under a spell. Y/N

4. Personal Questions

   Category 1: Magical and Paranormal Elements

  a) What kinds of things happened before or in the initial phases of the relationship that led you to believe that this was perhaps out of the ordinary? Things such as vivid dreams, astral connecting with the partner, synchronicities, a stronger psychic link with the partner than was normally experienced with anyone, etc. Explain.

  b) Did the relationship seem to be manipulated or orchestrated from unseen intelligences, and make you feel that you were under a spell?

  c) How did you feel the connection, did you have a greater degree of passion, and did you feel this to be more than just sexual? Did your heart area, solar plexus or other areas feel distinctly different? Describe.

  d) Did you experience a heightened degree of psychic sensitivity or empathy with your partner or other people during this love drama?

  e) Did you or your partner witness any ghostly presences, spirits, or alien entities during or immediately preceding the love relationship?

f) Did you or your partner experience a love obsession that was not characteristic for you or them?

Category 2: Emotional highs, lows, drama, emotional draining

a) Were you emotionally drained after a certain point, and did this affect you physically, like getting ill or losing a lot of weight?

b) Did events happen out of your control that kept you both from being able to meet or consummate the relationship or do more things together?

c) Did you find yourself thinking or doing things that was out of character for you when around this partner or even afterwards. Taking greater risks, for example.

d) Did you or your partner suddenly become emotionally switched off and uninterested for no apparent reason or was there a reason if this happened?

e) How long did it take you to heal and get over this love relationship? How long did the relationship last?

Category 3: Emotional Manipulation and the Psychopathology Element

a) Do you believe your partner was a psychopath, witch, demon influenced or possibly a possessed individual?

b) What kinds of behaviors did your partner do that you felt were:

- Emotionally manipulative, inflicting guilt, shame or that you are "less than" or "bad" Explain with an example.
- Controlling or abusive? Overt or passive-aggressive. Explain a typical scene or interaction.

In later chapters we will see just how these elements manifest within the dark side of Cupid relationship. This will become more apparent after exploring the case histories. We will then be better able to distinguish those attributes that are found within many normal "non-manipulated relationships" from those that are beyond the norm.

Chapter 5

# Case Files from The Dark Side of Cupid. Category One: Supernatural Influence and High Emotional Drama

Before venturing into the stories of my clients, I want to say a little more about the hallmarks of the Dark Side of Cupid experience. When examined from afar, the beginnings of the love drama appear positive, and perhaps within the normal range of human experience. But when delving deeper into the dynamics of the love match, I noticed that the experience held a greater degree of a magical reality. Overtones of extrasensory perception and paranormal elements manifested in ways that had not normally been experienced in the lovers' lives or in those of most people.

Many of the people who came to me regarding their unusual love relationship experience were perceptive, sensitive individuals. Some of them were healers, psychics, or intuitive in some capacity. Some believed they had been visited by extraterrestrials. Some came from mainstream walks of life, but who had encountered a love relationship with a powerful person, like a religious cult-like leader, or a famous and successful entrepreneur.

I want to make it clear that this type of relationship I've identified as a Dark Cupid match can happen to anyone. It can mask itself to make it appear that one has found their "soul mate," but upon deeper inspection and with time it reveals itself to be fool's gold. Later in this book, I will show examples of how the magical elements of a real soul mate match may be similar to a Dark Side of Cupid match, but how they differ in

## The Dark Side of Cupid

the quality of the relationship. Good soul mate matches lack the emotional draining, dramatic highs, crashing lows, and elements of emotional manipulation and psychopathology.

> **This type of relationship I've identified as a Dark Cupid match can happen to anyone. It can mask itself to make it appear that one has found their "soul mate," but upon deeper inspection and with time it reveals itself to be fool's gold.**

The stories that follow are categorized into four main sections, according to the severity of impact upon the partner who reported the love-connection experience. The first two cases exhibit the consensus that the love relationship was somehow staged from supernatural sources. In addition to this basic quality, the reporting partner experienced emotional highs and lows, as well as chaotic drama indicative of some form of emotional vampirism.

The second series of cases exhibit high drama and emotional vampirism where the person's partner was involved in channeling entities or was under the guidance of questionable spirit guides. These couples reported feeling as though their relationship had been orchestrated from such channeled entities in addition to experiencing a magical reality, as if they were playing a drama in mythic themes.

The third category contains those involving a more moderate form of emotional drama and psychic vampirism. In this case, a third party entity – such as a demon – is observed or suspected to be overshadowing the partner who has manipulative or psychopathic characteristics. The people who reported these cases believed not only that a supernatural source arranged their love affair, but influenced it throughout the relationship. The result was a certain degree of emotional exhaustion and paranormal activity.

The fourth category of stories represent more severe cases of energy vampirism. This is where one partner seems to be heavily overshadowed by an outside entity. This entity is suspected to be the culprit behind the manifestations of psychic vampirism, paranormal activity, and psychopathic behaviors in the partner, who is acting as an energy vampire. These couples also believed their relationship to be supernaturally set up and influenced throughout the entire duration of their love affair. Physical complaints such as solar plexus sensations and exhaustion are characteristic of psychic vampirism, as opposed to simple emotional vampirism. These cases demonstrate a greater degree of psychological injury.

The case histories represent the range of what is seen in my consulting practice. Supernatural interference may be anywhere from a nudging sense that "this love connection feels like it's being orchestrated elsewhere" to a hard-hitting realization that the lover is an outright "psychopathic, demonically overshadowed psychic vampire." The overriding sensation is that some kind of energy drain is taking place throughout the drama of the love affair. The energy drain can be understood as a form of energy vampirism. This can be experienced as emotional, psychic, or physical.

The energy drain is theorized as originating from Cupid, but as we shall see in the upcoming cases, Cupid may actually be some kind of interdimensional entity, an alien, a reptilian, demon, troll spirit, or simply a paranormal viral factor. These entities appear to be predatory in nature, based on the effect they have on the emotional and physical well being of the lovers. I believe that what we are seeing here is much more than a simple case of emotional or psychic vampirism. Although this may be what is taking place, its ultimate origin may be intedimensional in nature, not strictly the "fault" of one or the other partners. This is what differentiates the dark side of Cupid and the alien love bite from simple psychic vampirism. This feature also differentiates the dark side of Cupid from simple love affairs gone sour.

I would also like to point out the difference between an "alien love bite" and the dark side of Cupid love connection. The alien love bite is believed to be a love bond orchestrated by the alien beings who regularly interact with one or both partners, usually the person who is the "abductee." The dark side of Cupid, by contrast, is a love connection that is supernaturally arranged, interfered with, or influenced in such a way that some form of emotional or psychic vampirism takes place, usually via one partner who acts as the primary "energy vampire." In the dark side of Cupid, it is not entirely clear who these beings are because, as we shall see in the case histories, Cupid can take many forms.

The chapters following the four main categories of case histories represent variations on this theme. Two are cases where the couples experienced relationship interference in which their love connections were continuously disrupted or severed. The final case history chapter contains alien love bite cases from the archives of the late Barbara Bartholic. She shared three cases with me from 1998 of diabolical alien abductions where some form of love obsession ensued. These cases are on the far end of the spectrum, one of which resulted in suicide and others with disastrous psychological injury.

*Category One: Supernatural Influence and High Emotional Drama*

*Elizabeth and James*

Elizabeth, a mental health professional in her early forties, was living in the San Francisco Bay Area of California a few years prior to our interview. At that time she was looking for an affordable place to live that would enable her to build her home business as an artist.

When I asked her about any unusual experiences relating to the onset of her relationship with James, she answered,

"Before the relationship with James started I had just moved into a house that had many electrical malfunctions. My neighbors and I saw orbs and experienced poltergeist activity, and I had occasional night terrors. We had mysterious fires in our cable boxes more than once and the cable companies had to come to replace wires several times."

Elizabeth met James at work and they were scheduled to work together on several cases. Even in the first few weeks, Elizabeth started getting "that feeling" in her solar plexus and wasn't sure about James, but he seemed to work hard to establish a friendship with her. They worked together fairly regularly for the next two years, and developed a mutual artist friendship. She confided in James many difficulties she was having with office politics, and he was happy to give her advice. Elizabeth shared many of her insights and feelings, and came to trust James more readily.

Some of the problems Elizabeth had at work involved personality clashes with another female co-worker. When she confided in James, he told her, "Do you know why she hates you? Because of me! She's jealous because I like you better!"

James encouraged Elizabeth to actively fight with this aggressive and childish co-worker, but she refused to stoop to that level, preferring to take the high road and act like a professional adult. James was disappointed and continued to encourage her to fight with this co-worker, but Elizabeth believed it was his male ego viewing the situation, and didn't really take him seriously.

When I asked Elizabeth about unusual dreams, she told me, "James would meet me in my dreams and we would make love. This happened very often, after we had met and started working together. The dream astral sex was very nice and I felt like he was there with me all the time. When I brought this up with him much later, after approaching him for a relationship, he admitted he had felt the same way."

Because of these frequent astral sex dreams, Elizabeth

began having more sexual feelings for James. It was at this point that she approached him for a "friends with benefits" relationship. At first James was thrown for a loop. He seemed to be very concerned about whether Elizabeth was a "slut" and confided to Elizabeth about a painful break up he had years ago with a girlfriend who cheated on him behind his back with several of his friends. Finally, after a couple of months of this, James and Elizabeth went out on their first official date.

"We talked, and went out to town for a bite to eat. We kissed and BAM! Chemistry! Our first kiss was very powerful, as if a palpable beam of energy shot from my third eye forehead area to his. In fact, a few times it shot back so strongly that he jumped back. I had no control over this; it happened spontaneously. We went back to my place and kissed some more, but he refused to consummate it. He started having flashbacks of his ex-girlfriend, and wanted to take things slow with me, and have a real relationship. Then he told me of how a few years previously, an Indian holy man came into the shop where he used to work and gave him a prediction of how he would meet the woman of his dreams, the love of his life.

"Suddenly, I remembered having had a vision of an odd looking Indian man near a place where I used to work. He looked ancient, and wore his hair in dread locks. I wondered if it was the same man. But I also felt a little confused and alarmed."

Since it seemed that they had similar visions, Elizabeth thought, "maybe it's true! Soul mates!"

James assured her after the first date that they would get together soon. But weeks and a few months went by without close contact with him – not even for a cup of coffee. Elizabeth was perplexed as to why James seemed to avoid having real physical contact, and events out of their control seemed to prevent them getting from together.

Elizabeth explained, "Of course later, I realized it was him being evasive of being physically intimate – or even just real friends."

At the same time, Elizabeth was still having astral sex dreams with James, but these were incongruent with his evasive behavior at work. It was as if he were experiencing an inner conflict of mixed emotions; he even threw a tantrum at work one day. James avoided her and they did not see each other for six months. Then one day at work, James approached Elizabeth and they later engaged in deep kissing briefly. Everything seemed wonderful, and they planned on setting another date to see a movie together. But by the next week James reverted back to his angry, jealous self like a Jekyll-Hyde switch and when they kissed again, he exhibited aggressive and dominant sexual behavior that made Elizabeth nervous. Following this incident were several more months of minimal contact.

Elizabeth was so perplexed by this relationship she consulted several psychics, some who urged her to break it off with James and others who perpetuated the situation, saying he was her soul mate.

Elizabeth decided to confront James about his evasiveness and pretending to want to be together, as well as his redundant surface level conversations and his avoidance of real life connections. She cut it off with him and told him to stop calling her. Meanwhile, however, the sexual dreams and psychic connection continued, and Elizabeth intuitively felt as if James wanted to keep the sexual dream fantasy connection. He had mentioned to her earlier that he was well aware of the astral sex liaisons, as if he could do this at will – a form of psychic dream walking. The endless drama caused Elizabeth's emotions to yo-yo up and down, and soon she felt drained, but not ill, and mostly distracted from her work.

Elizabeth recalls, "Our love obsession was not typical for him or me."

After a few months Elizabeth heard via co-workers that James made mean comments associating her with other women in an angry, misogynistic tone. She felt insulted that James so easily threw her in the same bandwagon as her co-workers, as if her entire identity revolved around her work. His shallow perception shocked and hurt her. Around that same time, Elizabeth felt a heavy pain in her neck, like a sword chop, and intuitively she knew something had changed in James. Now, she noticed, the astral sex dreams ceased and it was as if James no longer had a psychic hold on her. But then after a few days, Elizabeth could feel James wanting to reconnect psychically. He emailed a few times apologizing and wanted to re-establish their connection. Elizabeth refused and called him an incubus.

Then, ironically, within days a flurry of male attention came out of the woodwork at Elizabeth, and she found herself surrounded by men wanting to get to know her. She sensed something supernatural was up but kept it to herself. Simultaneously her co-workers changed their attitude towards her at work and Elizabeth's supervisor suddenly became cold.

After a few months of not responding to the other men and not reacting to her co-workers' changed attitudes, Elizabeth received text messages from James again. More self-aware and made wiser by what she could now see as the endless emotional drama hooks, Elizabeth decided not to respond. In hindsight, she believes her relationship with James veered her away from her path in life by keeping her distracted from her creative work.

*Anna and Kaleb*

Anna, a wife and mother in her thirties living on the East Coast, USA, came to me following a series of life altering experiences including a powerful love relationship that she believed to be orchestrated by otherworldly sources. She understood herself to be an experiencer of alien encounters, and believes this relationship to have been set up by her alien visitors. Anna had also been trying to patch up her 16-year

*Chapter 5: Case Files from the Dark Side of Cupid*

marriage after her husband admitted to an affair with another woman. But, he swore, he had broken it off and promised to work on the marriage.

During this worrisome time, Anna met Kaleb, an Australian man four years older than she, on an Internet discussion forum. Unknown to Anna, Kaleb had been searching for a girl he had seen in his dreams decades earlier, whom he knew deep in his soul was a real person he was destined to meet later in life, by way of some sort of machine. Throughout his teen years, Kaleb had several dreams of meeting with Anna, but for him they were not merely dreams, but something more real, perhaps astral meetings in the dreamtime.

Anna recalled her first impressions of Kaleb while meeting online. "There was something vaguely familiar about Kaleb; perhaps it was his demeanor or sensitivity that initially got my attention. But there was also a strange magnetism that I couldn't deny. He had posted a mild complaint about a different research site that many of us had abrasive feedback from. I felt the strong urge to add my two cents in a supportive manner and in doing so ended up striking up a conversation with him. The topic of conversation immediately became very personal so we opted to talk in a private way away from the rest of the group. That was when Kaleb decided to put the question to me: "Do you remember a place of green rolling hills, the purest white fluffy clouds and lots of enormous smiles?"

What seemed like a simple question created an eruption of emotional rock and ash that quickly settled in and around me and threatened to suffocate me. I tentatively responded with, "Yes and there was another boy in the dream as well as a huge shadow that fell across us, and energies emanating from this shadow somehow transformed us, leaving us tingling and consciously altered – do you remember?"

There was a measured silence on Kaleb's end, after Anna recalled more details to a forgotten dream she had nearly 27 years ago.

"Yes, yes! We had been practicing mental exercises with each other including telepathy, teleportation and telekinesis just before the shadow fell. I don't know what hovered above us in order that a shadow should be thrown, but I strongly remember at that moment not wanting us to be parted and having a forewarning that this was to be."

Anna remembers:

> "I repeatedly asked Kaleb after moments of silence, 'Kaleb? Are you there?'
>
> 'Yes,' Kaleb answered.
>
> 'What's wrong?' I asked, not sure what to expect.
>
> 'Nothing.' He typed, 'I'm just trying to take all of this in.
>
> 'Kaleb, how did you know about that valley?' I asked, wanting him to tell me it was all some kind of coincidence, and that he was somehow joking.
>
> 'Anna, I was there.' Kaleb affirmed.
>
> 'How can this be?' I punched in the keyboard. His response wasn't what I had expected.
>
> 'I'm not sure,' he said, 'but I have been looking for you for the past 27 years!'"

Anna now became so stunned and agitated with excitement that she felt ill. These memories went beyond her normal capacity to feel, and she started to feel numb.

She asked Kaleb, "What do you mean you've been looking for me for 27 years?"

"I don't know." Kaleb said with a tangible sadness, "I just have."

Then he typed, "I always knew that was a real experience and not a dream, and that someday I would find you. I had a vision of a machine that would one day bring us together and there was no way then that I could have known it was the computer and the Internet that I had seen in my vision and that it was this machine that would be the catalyst."

It was at this moment that Anna started to feel a stronger

magnetic pull towards Kaleb, as the drawing became more of a physical sensation that she couldn't deny or comprehend. She wanted to take a few steps back to talk about this unbelievable revelation. For what Kaleb described to her was a vivid lucid dream experience she had when she was about 11 years old.

Anna told Kaleb, "It isn't possible for you to even know how to describe those unusual details unless you were indeed there."

> **'Kaleb, how did you know about that valley?' I asked, wanting him to tell me it was all some kind of coincidence, and that he was somehow joking. 'Anna, I was there,' Kaleb affirmed.**

Simultaneously Anna became aware and actually felt his emotional turmoil inside manifesting in her heart center. From this point on Anna and Kaleb felt so connected that it was beyond her ability fully to comprehend. She later decided that she was somehow connecting with Kaleb on the inside – a deep soul connection.

Anna continued, "Since I had never experienced anything quite like this before, I was able to fend off the sensations until that moment in time. It was as if our separate energy fields, long invisible tentacles, had suddenly developed and were reaching out through inner space to entwine with each other. It was as if we were two people pulling towards each other in order to occupy one heart."

The ability to connect with each other's feelings and thoughts grew as Anna and Kaleb continued their correspondence. It was the first time Anna experienced real telepathy and a powerful, passionate soul connection to such a degree. Not only were they able to become aware of one another's emotional state and thoughts, but also Anna experienced

*The Dark Side of Cupid*

telesthesia.*

Anna and Kaleb stayed in contact by email and telephone for a year and a half until they decided it was time to meet. At the time, each one had been having marital issues with their respective partners and contemplated severing marital ties to explore the possibility of being together. This would be their chance to meet and get to know one another more deeply, and at least to figure out what really happened in those lucid dreamscapes twenty-seven years before.

Kaleb's business in Australia was considering a move to an office in the USA, perhaps New York, which was exciting news to Anna. Perhaps they would have a chance to see one another more often, and were meant to be. They decided to meet at a resort hotel in Hawaii, to meet in person for the first time.

However, they had built up such excitement and tension prior to meeting, that when the moment finally happened, they were overcome with an uneasy, anxious, feeling. The consummation of their deep soul connection did occur, but with a tense discomfort. The ten-day rendezvous of a lifetime quest fell short when Kaleb received a call from his wife that his young daughter was ill. He had to leave the next day. On top of it all, he learned that his company had decided not to move to New York after all.

Anna was devastated. What had been an emotional buildup of an incredibly deep connection, sexual longing, and passionate excitement to connect and possibly have a future with this man, was cut short all in one afternoon.

Kaleb left three days before his scheduled departure, leaving Anna alone for the remainder of the Hawaiian vacation. During the entire plane flight back, Anna cried, her hopes

---

\* This is a term coined by Ingo Swann, well-known psychic and remote viewer, and author of *Psychic Sexuality* [Ingo Swann, 1999]. Telesthesia is the ability to perceive and even physically sense another person's energy field, especially when one person is sexually fantasizing about the other.

and dreams crushed. Not only had she been betrayed by her husband, who admitted to having an affair earlier that year, but she had been rejected by Kaleb, a man she had the most powerful soul bond with, even stronger than she had ever felt with her husband. After the tears cleared, and after Anna had time to reflect, she realized that Kaleb had gotten scared. He realized he could not leave his family for her. It just wasn't meant to be.

The upheaval in Anna's life was a time of sorrow, change, and growth. She and her husband of 17 years divorced, and she became a statistic: another poor single mother struggling to recapture a lost career and income earning potential, now barely surviving in poverty. Others may have not fared as well as she in dealing with and healing from this profound, emotionally devastating loss.

I asked her what it was that helped her maintain her strength and move forward with such bold confidence. She replied, "because I walked the shamanic path, I learned how to read and sense energy at an early age, and decided to follow the light and wisdom of nature. These sensitivities helped me become aware of the darker realms as well and assisted me in my self-realization and empowerment as a lesson of greater awareness."

Chapter 6

# Category Two: Mythic Dramas, Spirit Guides and Emotional Vampirism

The stories in this chapter exhibit high emotional drama, and the feeling that the love affair was supernaturally staged by a source, in particular the spirit guides being channelled by one of the partners. These couples felt as though their relationships were mythic dramas being played out, in which they truly felt the sensation of being in a magical reality. However, the partner who channeled the spirit guides also manifested emotional vampire tendencies.

*Nathan and Jezebel*

Nathan shared with me key points of an unusual relationship he had with a woman named Jezebel. In his own words, "when we first met, some form of recognition was immediately present. The first thing she said was something like, 'Well, where have you been all my life?' I responded similarly and we immediately felt we had known each other a very long time. She was a beautiful woman and so I thought I had finally found my one and future partner for this lifetime."

Soon after meeting Jezebel, he experienced an unusually strong psychic link with her — more than he had ever experienced with anyone else. Their connection felt deep, even though they had only just met. After the initial meeting, Nathan accepted her invitation to attend a New Age-related lecture, even though it involved a drive of several hours. During the long drive, he started receiving mental images and impressions of black hooded figures and burning at the stake. These impressions, according to Nathan, felt as if they were dropped into his mind, but he also thought they might be powerful past life memories.

## Chapter 6: Case Files, Category Two

"I had constant feelings of being in a magical state of reality with this woman. We both had heightened feelings of romantic connection, almost non-stop feelings of romantic love and fascination, but never any sex. I became aware of something strange, as if she was afraid of getting too close to me. I had a sense that she felt she could continue to control me if we didn't have sex, but would lose control if we did. I wondered if perhaps by having sex, my energies would threaten her."

Nathan and Jezebel shared many conversations in person and by telephone. Despite the lack of sexual intimacy, Nathan felt strongly enough about Jezebel to continue seeing her. He had Tarot readings and the I Ching telling him that he had met his ideal spiritual partner. He was mesmerized by her.

But there was a less appealing side to this relationship. He noticed she seemed to be constantly surrounded by men, who followed her around like puppy dogs. In addition, he said they both explored the possibility of having had former lifetimes together, "a karmic connection where psychics told us we shared lifetimes, where I had done harm to her, was responsible for her being murdered – burned at the stake – and that now I had to beg for forgiveness."

Eventually, Nathan started to feel as if he was being "played" by this woman to be manipulated into subjugation by her, groveling for her approval, affections, and forgiveness.

Nathan explains, "I felt emotionally whiplashed to an extraordinary degree over and over again."

Nathan also began to feel odd sensations in his solar plexus, as if an unseen entity wanted to attach itself to him. He also began to have a different sense of himself. He suddenly preferred to wear black, and his friends commented that he became very serious and dark. Nathan told me, "Under her thrall I got worse and worse. Others around me started noticing that I was changing and my dearest friend and teacher became very worried and asked me, 'Are you ok?'"

In general, Nathan found that events always happened in

such a way to prevent consummation of his desire for her while at the same time deepen Jezebel's control over him. "On the surface," he said, "she seemed very loving and warm, but when I got close and we had a chance to be alone, then instead of feeling a warm closeness, I felt an icy distance. The entire relationship with this woman was strange, as if the channeled entities she communicated with were running the entire show. To make matters worse, she did something that surprised me. In a conversation one night, out of the blue she just up and mentioned that she had a new boyfriend, the way someone might announce they just bought a new refrigerator. I was absolutely shattered by her casual mention of this while I thought she was still very interested in me."

By this time Nathan was so hurt by her unusual behaviors that he mulled it over, grieving and praying. His gut instinct told him, "this whole thing does not make sense." He added, "the entire experience was enormously all-encompassing emotionally to the point I was just exhausted by it all and in the end just wanted to get away from it."

When I asked Nathan how long it took to disengage emotionally and heal from the experience, his response reiterated the entire "magical and paranormal nature" of the love drama. He recalled, "in the beginning and into the next few months of the relationship things got worse, and at that point I began to develop an inner suspicious nature of the whole relationship. It was just a gut feeling that something unnatural and weird was going on."

Nathan's prayers received answers in ways that confirmed his suspicions that this woman was dangerous. This young lady, while looking like an angel, operated more like a one-person demonic hierarchy! Paradoxically, after thinking things over, Nathan lost all obsessive feelings for her. His hurt feelings vanished within a few hours' time, as if they had never even been there.

"I was amazed," he related with awe. "I expected to at least

> **The entire relationship with this woman was strange, as if the channeled entities she communicated with were running the entire show.**

need weeks or months to heal, but the entire obsession vanished almost completely. It was that experience that made me really begin to wonder what was going on. In other words, it was a completely atypical response to being hurt."

Nathan reflected back on that time when he had completely broken all romantic ties, as if waking from a dream. He walked around asking himself, "What kind of spell was I under?"

*Kundra and Stan*

Kundra, a vibrant, sensuous thirty-something writer and psychic, began her own desktop publishing magazine about alternative healing, spirituality, and environmentally conscientious issues. In the midst of her publishing enterprise and doing public talks about her alternative energy healing practice, she met Stan. Unknown to Kundra, Stan heard in a Tarot reading that he was supposed to find his twin flame and leave his wife.

At first Kundra wasn't sexually attracted to Stan, and yet they shared a strong connection with one another and later they became sexually involved after getting to know one another. Kundra told me, "My life was already highly spiritual, and I appeared to people, giving them Shaktipat healing energy, in person and sometimes out of the body. This energy could reach them (in both ways). I did that with him, and he had very powerful results."

Kundra mentioned that during this time there were definitely unusual things happening, and she believed this to be at least in part due to the effects of sending Shaktipat healing energy. Stan said that after she sent energy, he experienced his bed covers rise off of him by themselves, as if lifted by unseen hands.

"He continued to have physical effects happen at night, such as his covers rising off of him, and I wasn't sure what was going on. His trances and Tarot readings were saying we were meant to be together. It seemed epic, magical, like what I had been waiting for, though almost nothing about him really fit what I had been looking for."

Stan would go into trance on occasion, and communicate with his spirit guides. Kundra explains, "We were led by his spirit guides, whom he channeled to do certain magic rituals. The guides wanted me to have a child with him, but I refused. He actually set up to include me in Egyptian magical rituals which I learned later were for me to fall in love with him. He was intelligent, handsome, strong, charismatic and very much in love with me. We were told and believed at the time (that) we had a special magical mission to do together that involved helping free the world from the state of dominion it is under – evil control."

Eventually, their relationship became sexually intense. "Our lovemaking was earth shattering," Kundra related. "He and I had such a bond that being apart for a minute was painful. We pledged our love forever, and I was going to marry him, which was bizarre for me, and I got to where I wouldn't even look at other men at all, like a woman in Afghanistan, just to placate him. It was like I was always about to lose him in the abyss or something, so that our love was extra desperate."

Stan was torn apart by frequent attacks of unfounded jealousy. He was channeling entities that Kundra felt were evil. He went through sudden changes of perspective and at times she thought he was going insane. Kundra recalls:

"We played out dramas of intense battles, male versus female, good versus evil, controller versus controlled; like being thrown into a magical drama led by his spirit guides. It was like being inserted into a mythic drama of Isis and Osiris, the divine couple.

"Our love was filled with omens, signs, and synchronicities that had been planned all our lives. Or so it seemed at the time. It was the only time I really felt I was with a twin flame, and ever had that desperate need to be with someone so strongly, and it was the same with him. And throughout this entire relationship, and even afterwards, I dreamed of being with him and lovemaking. The connection was unreal.

"The entities that he channeled seemed to siphon off of our memories, sexual energies, and powers and put in something new. They waited until things were great, building up more energy through wonderful sex and love and accomplishments, and then took it out. He then became forgetful, as if memories were taken out and then he would become distant and impossible to deal with."

Kundra became exhausted after these dramas took place, and developed chronic fatigue syndrome. Throughout this time Stan's wife prevented him from divorcing her, so that he and Kundra could not marry. According to Kundra, "the dramas we were placed in, that seemed beyond our control and somehow orchestrated by his entities, had the effect of making our love obsession stronger. He was always going to be killed or some other nerve-wracking possibility. He later became switched off from me emotionally. Suddenly."

When asked to describe more about her energy loss and healing work, Kundra had a lot to say.

"Sometimes when I've helped a person with healing, using a lot of my willpower that way, my lower back would go out, and my kidneys would have problems. Of course now, I know to listen to these symptoms and I have learned to keep my boundaries and self-respect. I do not allow myself to be hurt if possible and I value my health and well-being much more than before. When healing others in my work, I will only work with them when they are helping themselves, and not too much in a self-sacrificing way."

I agreed with Kundra, and added that as women, I believe we often give too much in relationships and must learn to pull back our gifts of energies and do more self-nurturing, because if we don't, it backfires.

Kundra shared more about this.

"Our conditioning convinces us it's ok to give away our energy too much because we are supposed to care for others, are too lazy, timid, or weak to fight back. We feel we have to be conditionally loved this way, to do good for the world. We may have addictions because of this, because we allow ourselves to believe deceits because of religion, subliminal messages or whatever it is. In a way, even this is part of the Dark Side of Cupid – its web of interconnections. Like being brought up in a family in which it's ok for the father to mistreat the mother, being in a country where all our rights are being taken away and few stand up to fight, being caught up having to struggle to make a living all the time, lending money to people who don't repay, helping others because we are made to feel guilty, and giving up adrenalin for the sake of entertainment."

Kundra later considered that Stan may have been possessed by dark entities, or perhaps was pretending to be possessed. She admitted to having felt taken in by this man, but at the same time felt that she and Stan were irresistibly in love with one another. There appeared to be archetypal forces and synchronicities beyond the visible world directing their almost mythical drama. It was extremely difficult to resist the love affair.

"If I could reflect on what happened with Stan," Kundra added, "it was as if his resistance to a more positive, unselfish spiritual path and relationship was represented by the negative entities and "reptilians" who, metaphorically, manifested as his "dwellers on the threshold." They manipulated into dominance that aspect of his human nature that resists the raising of awareness."

The impact of the effects of the Dark Side of Cupid cannot be underestimated. The relationship between Kundra and Stan lasted less than a year, yet it took her sixteen years to heal from this love bite.

In Kundra's words, "that whole experience with Stan was impossible to really ever categorize and fully understand its power over me, years of mystification. I've never felt I was taken in like that (again) to such a degree with other men – at all. My other life experiences have been more empowering as a whole. I've had other relationships later in life that I've suspected were manipulated but now at least I'm able to perceive it, question it, and most people don't even have that awareness."

I wonder, is this some kind of drama enacted by ancient mythological gods for the sake of learning, or is it something else? It's something I do think long and hard about. I know I'm not alone in this.

*Jeremy and Clive*

Jeremy, a single gay man in his mid-forties, had within the last six months seriously started studying global government conspiracies, extraterrestrial races, spirituality, and metaphysical subjects. He had a casual interest in these topics beforehand, but became more intent on exploring them. He met Clive, another single gay man at his place of employment, where they both began a friendship, which turned more intimate as time went by.

I asked Jeremy if he experienced anything unusual, paranormal or synchronistic prior to or in the initial stages of seeing Clive.

"The most significant coincidence in the beginning," he said, "was his display of deep knowledge and apparent insight into esoteric subjects I had just finished studying regarding extraterrestrial and interdimensional races, as well as spiritual and metaphysical pursuits. I would have completely dismissed him had there not been a foundation to base the relationship on. He also had the ability to reveal intimate details of my life, including those of close friends and family that no one else would know. He also said we were spirit mates, but it was entirely up to me if we bonded as such."

As Jeremy got to know Clive more intimately, he discovered that Clive regularly communicated with spirit guides whom he also channeled. Clive told him these entities were benevolent reptilians and our creators from the 8th dimension. Over a decade before, said Clive, he had been approached consciously by these interdimensional guides, after which his life began to fall apart. Jeremy discovered that Clive had endured a difficult childhood and significant trauma and torture from some alien visitations and military-type abductions. He also told Jeremy about intermittent attacks by dark forces, as if this were some kind of training the aliens tested him with. Clive suffered from sleep disturbances and acute physical pains as a result. Clive often referred to his interdimensional guides as "The Council of Twelve."

Jeremy later discovered from Clive's spirit guides that the reptilian entities arranged his relationship with Clive in order to heal Clive of his ailments and sleep deprivation, as well as aiding Clive in the ascension process. Jeremy was told that he would also benefit from this process but would only realize this once he stepped through it. Oddly enough, whenever Jeremy asked the spirit guides questions about why he was being asked to do certain things, he was usually told to stop asking, and all would be revealed once the scenario was fulfilled, and simply to trust them.

The guides told Jeremy that they had been watching him for a very long time, and over many lifetimes. These entities were particularly interested in his interaction with Clive to see what happened. Apparently many alien groups were monitoring Clive and Jeremy, and everything was being recorded due to the special interest in what they described as a rare or unique situation. The guides told them that they had been lovers in many previous lives and this would be the last opportunity to bond before ascending. They were told there would be infinite potential if the bond were to occur. The roles were varied in previous lives and references to Atlantis were made. Jeremy was told that he would have a leadership role in an uncertain global apocalyptic future and meet others like himself.

Jeremy admitted to feeling a connection with Clive before they became more physically intimate. In fact, his libido shot through the roof, and became heightened during this time, although his libido wasn't necessarily directed towards Clive. But after bonding, Jeremy didn't consider the sexual contact to be particularly intense, rewarding, or intimate. Jeremy's lack of feelings for him disappointed Clive, who soon started acting resentful.

I asked Jeremy whether he experienced significant emotional highs and crashing lows with Clive, and whether he became emotionally or physically drained in his presence.

"I most definitely experienced emotional highs and lows," he replied, "primarily due to the corroboration or clarification I received from him on the esoteric knowledge I had been studying. I felt tremendous pressure to apply this knowledge in constructive ways, especially as directed by Clive's guides, to participate in helping us to fulfill an unspoken contract with them. I did feel we were being thrown around from one drama to the next as the guides were directing Clive, and thus he was directing me, in what was required to accommodate a scenario with the intent of bonding emotionally and energetically. There was an implied element of consent through free will, but a tremendous amount of external pressure to perform to a certain spiritual ideal and level of expectation, as the guides were continually offering feedback to both of us. I felt both emotionally and physically drained when with him and during this relationship."

Clive told Jeremy that his guides had questions about the strength of the bonding, as Clive said that a weak bond would inhibit him from pulling Jeremy through an interdimensional portal when the time came. The guides told Clive that his physical ailments and sleep deprivation would end when they bonded and this clearly did not happen. Nor did Jeremy want to be with Clive as much as Clive wanted to be with him. Jeremy found it unsettling and incongruent that the interdimensional beings were supposed to be benevolent, considering Clive's poor health, constant sleep disturbances, and explosive anger issues. It made no sense. This led Jeremy to start questioning the truthfulness of the channeled spirit messages.

"The guides told Clive certain things that would happen to him and they didn't," Jeremy said. "His condition and demeanor continued to deteriorate when we were together. When I questioned them about it, they replied that they manipulated certain things for his benefit so he wouldn't quit his mission and veer off course. Clive was in a lot of emotional and physical turmoil, not being able to sleep for several years due to his trauma and interaction with the guides. It didn't make sense that a powerful benevolent race couldn't assist Clive in a more humane way; especially considering all the technology they apparently had. His life also completely fell apart after his initial contact with these beings even though they reported to be protecting him."

I asked Jeremy whether Clive had manipulative or abusive ways of interacting with him.

Jeremy replied that Clive "was manipulative and abusive, demonstrating mannerisms incongruent with his message and desire to help everyone. He most notably became intensely controlling, and demanded almost everything I do to be according to his specifications and approval. He was controlling beyond anyone I'd seen, and his outbursts were out of control and completely disproportionate to any perceived cause, as he demonstrated contempt and rage towards me, and most people we met, resenting anyone he perceived as being weak. In the beginning, I was told he would love me no matter what, but this was clearly not the case, as he continued to be self-absorbed with his pain, his story, and his mission. The guides also told him that I was his "equal" but that didn't carry very far with him. Compassion was only demonstrated when it meant he would be the focus of a person's admiration, further fueling his narcissism."

I wondered what kinds of alien visitations Clive had to cause him to act in ways that exhibited a kind of Stockholm syndrome, as well as being emotionally abusive in his relationships. If the reptilian guides were so benevolent, then why all the problems? I also asked Jeremy whether he had experienced any alien visitations in his life, and he firmly said no. However, he admitted to a few unusual dreams.

"I had several dreams," he said, "where I interacted with three beings who appeared to me in various forms, like three women or three black men. Clive offered clarification after I mentioned this to him, saying that the three women were reptilian nurses who he had also interacted with. They were apparently consulting with me for feedback on my experiences and also reportedly removed something from me. Clive was also involved extensively in what he called training exercises in other realms during the early mornings where he appeared to be asleep but was fully conscious."*

Clive also had shared with Jeremy more details about what the reptilian guides were doing to him during his "abductions." His guides told Clive that they were preparing a new astral body – he referred to it as a multidimensional body – built by the reptilians, who were to transfer him into it when the time

---

* These are commonly reported by abductees and milabs and what we now call "stage managed dreams."

was right. Clive said he remembered being transported on many occasions to special labs where procedures were performed by benevolent beings to remove disease and upgrade or implant devices in his body. Clive was told all this was being done in preparation for a final spiritual confrontation with a powerful malevolent entity, and that he would be head of a legion to do battle against dark forces. The reptilians told Clive they were adding upgrades into his body and certain chakra points.

I asked Jeremy whether he thought Clive's spirit guides were deceptive and, if so, what kind of false information was being related.

"I feel the guides are deceiving Clive," said Jeremy, "since he is rapidly deteriorating through this process and they told him several things that have not happened or have been inaccurate. Clive's rationale always fell into the category of cognitive dissonance.* They are not as benevolent as they report to be (by their fruits ye shall know them) and they have a far subtler agenda at play because they refused to answer many questions."

Finally, I asked him how long it took to heal from this relationship, and whether or not his belief systems changed as a result of it.

He replied, "I am still healing from this relationship, since it entailed leaving my job, home, friends and family. My views have been shifted or reinforced in that I now know through experience that many of these New Age organizations/themes, especially those involving Ascension/2012 End Times, are being infiltrated, staged and manipulated for a far more subtle and insidious agenda. Truth mixed with lies to primarily appeal to

---

\* The discomfort someone feels when having two conflicting cognitions. It is notable that this term was created by author Leon Festinger in his 1956 book, *When Prophecy Fails*, which chronicled the followers of a UFO cult, as reality clashed with their fervent beliefs of an impending apocalypse. See http://www.en.wikipedia.org/wiki/Cognitive_dissonance

a person's ego and further disempower them. The next level of consciousness awareness that many call being spiritual are plagued with even more sophisticated traps that cleverly match your new expanding awareness."

This is something that has happened to many I have consulted over the years. It is sad to see so much energy and attention being placed on fashionable New Age trends, where many contactees and channelers enjoy a high profile status on various radio shows and speaking venues. Then their victims come to me, to relate the real story and life behind those who claim to have contact with benevolent extraterrestrial guides. For many who have experienced the alien love bite, this love drama served to wake them up to a much grander reality in which humanity seems to be a pawn on a much larger chessboard, one full of ancient extraterrestrial gods fighting for ownership over human souls.

Chapter 7

# Category Three: Emotional Vampirism and Third Party Entities

These cases represent couples that either suspected or observed a third party entity, such as a demon or interdimensional entity, overshadowing or influencing their lover. These cases experienced high drama that is characteristic of emotional vampirism.

*Francine and Burt*

Francine, an attractive forty-something divorcee, wanted to meet someone new. Disappointed with the quality of men approaching her on an online dating site, she switched to an internet social networking site and met a man named Burt whom she found appealing. She posted friendly comments on his page, and let him know she wanted to meet him if he was in her part of town. Surprisingly enough, Burt responded, and seemed to have an attraction for Francine as well. He soon agreed to visit her.

Online, they seemed to have a lot in common, especially their views on spirituality and approaching life from a heart-centered standpoint. Francine thought Burt was sexy, good-looking, and close to her age, unlike the older men responding to her online dating profile. When Burt agreed to visit, Francine was excited but nervous, as he would be staying at her home instead of meeting at a café or public place. She hoped that even if he stayed in the extra bedroom, they would have a chance to get to know one another as friends, and then see where it would go.

When asked if there was anything magical or paranormal about Burt, Francine could only think that she sometimes "felt him" when in her afternoon meditations or spontaneous

*Chapter 7: Case Files, Category Three*

moments, as if he were perhaps thinking of her too. But it was only after they got together that the real strangeness began.

Burt arrived in the evening, and Francine made a light dinner for him. After talking for several hours that night, Burt suggested Francine give him a massage, and he reminded her that she offered to do this on a post she sent him online over a month prior. She didn't recall that, other than having mentioned to him she owned a massage table and had done Reiki healing in the past. Francine said the massage table was packed away and Burt would have to help her retrieve it from the storage closet. Seeing that it would be a bit of a hassle, Burt decided he could just lie on the king-sized bed in the master bedroom while she gave him a massage. He had driven for many hours and had tight muscles, he said.

Francine felt uncomfortable with his insistence on a massage, but decided to go ahead and give him one, anyway. Before she knew it, they were having sex. It happened so fast, but Francine decided she would just enjoy the intimacy, as it had been a while since she had been with a man. They fell asleep in each other's arms, and spent the next several days together. Most of the time while with Francine, Burt spent an inordinate amount of time on his laptop eagerly reading emails and reviewing the responses on his networking site. Francine passed it off as his busy lifestyle. "It was nice cooking for a man again," she admitted, "and having someone to sleep and cuddle with at night."

Before Burt left, they embraced and she gave him a goodbye kiss, hoping they would reconnect in the near future.

The night after Burt left town, Francine went to bed alone, still feeling aglow with his presence as she drifted off to sleep. However, she was abruptly awakened by a startling invisible presence. She felt it as a strong male energy whose astral body tried to hover over her sexually and meld with her body. This felt as if it were physically present, yet invisible. The entity even spoke to her in Burt's voice, with demeaning profanity that shocked her.

Panic-stricken and feeling ashamed, Francine got up immediately and turned on the light. She saw nothing, but still felt a presence. Whoever that entity was, it was pretending to be Burt but was acting like a demon. Francine was frightened.

She told me, "I figured the demonic entity attack must have been a coincidence and I gave Burt the benefit of the doubt that it wasn't connected to him. But Burt did other things that started making me feel uncomfortable, like continuing to be 'looking for his soul mate' with public posts to that effect on his networking page. He posted a photo of a woman he claims he fell in love with a few months before I met him online. I was crushed. I figured I wasn't the one he wanted to really be with and that I wasn't special to him at all."

But Francine let this incident go, because Burt was calling every day or so, and she said she could feel a heart connection to him, as if they were connected on a deeper soul level. He seemed to have a sixth sense about her thoughts and posted things that he would do to become a better man and to get in shape, and how he didn't sleep with 99% of the women who dated him because he only wanted his soul mate. It was a very romantic idea and Francine fell for it, hoping she would be the one for him.

They continued talking by phone and Francine decided to ask Burt about how he felt about her, and if he wanted to see her again. Burt was evasive, but Francine got him to talk. He confessed that he was confused, but still wanted to keep in contact. He could not really know his feelings until they had spent more time together, and he wanted to take it slow. Francine was okay with that, and admitted to being uncertain herself. Still, she was happy to remain in touch, even if by phone, but with the expectation that they would meet again sooner rather than later.

Meanwhile, Francine had intermittent night time visitations by the invisible entity that kept trying to meld with her energy body in a sexual manner. She resisted and prayed nightly because this was downright creepy and alarming. Francine emphasized that these were not dreams, "but something different." She felt strongly that the entity seemed connected to Burt, "in response to my thoughts and feelings about him. But it wasn't just that. If I had strong feelings, doubts or thoughts about him, his posts the next day or a text message would pop up regarding the same things I had been thinking about. Several times while I was thinking about him, he called."

But the phone calls were not enough to keep her feeling connected. Moreover, Burt expressed no interest in her beyond a "friends with benefits" interaction. Within a month, Francine was starting to detach, feeling that the connection between them should die a natural death. Silently, in her heart, she let Burt go, although didn't tell him anything.

As if Burt had a sixth sense, however, he called her the next evening. He was driving through the general area, he said, and was only a two or three hour drive away. He suggested he could come by and visit, as long as she would be willing to help with the extra gas money it would require. Francine hesitated. She had several appointments over the next few days, she told him, and wasn't sure. Maybe in the next week or so, she might be more free.

But her resolve faltered. Earlier, by phone, she had promised to make him a special birthday dinner if he was in town. She thought she might just go ahead and cancel a few appointments to make time for Burt. Burt chimed in that he was ready to take the exit so he needed to know soon, and that maybe it was best to allow the spontaneous moment to decide

> **Francine emphasized that these were not dreams, "but something different." She felt strongly that the entity seemed connected to Burt.**

– perhaps this was meant to be. Francine agreed, and soon Burt was on his way to her house.

He arrived very late that night, so tired he could barely keep his eyes open. Francine offered him a small meal, and after Burt ate, as if in a trance, he said he was so tired he wanted to go to bed. First, however, he asked for another massage. She went ahead and gave him a massage but he was so tired that he fell asleep before they could do any lovemaking.

The following morning, Burt again expressed no interest in sex, and instead wanted breakfast! Francine felt rejected. She enjoyed cooking, but began to feel that Burt didn't really care for her at all. They spent the next afternoon together, as he typed away on his laptop answering online messages. When they parted, Burt didn't even want to kiss Francine and only hugged her good-bye.

"After that," said Francine, "I felt pretty certain that Burt was not the man for me. I felt essentially rejected. But I still hung on to a thread of hope that maybe it was just bad timing, and if Burt wasn't so tired from all his travels that maybe we would have hit it off better. After all, we really did share a lot in common, and I seemed to be able to tune into him empathically so easily and he with me, almost in a supernatural way."

*Emotional Ping Pong Game*

Over the next few days, Burt posted on his networking page a declaration of love for a woman who was obviously not Francine. She lamented, "I felt like I was kicked in the teeth. It was almost as if he did it purposely just to elicit a hurtful response. Either that or he was extremely insensitive to how it would make a woman feel, one whom he had just shared intimacy with. I felt like I had allowed myself to lose all self-respect by sleeping with this man, who I thought could have been my soul mate. Boy was I wrong!"

*Chapter 7: Case Files, Category Three*

Francine decided that she needed to share her feelings about Burt's public posts, and so she sent him a private message after he had posted the declaration of love for this other woman. Francine told him she lost all romantic feelings and could only be friends from now on. She cried and decided to let the whole thing go as one big mistake. Then, when she was thinking strongly about Burt one evening after her private message to him, he called. But Francine didn't want to answer and let it go to her answering machine.

Later that night and for the next several nights, Francine received visits from the invisible entity. She felt its presence as angry and intrusive and she fought to keep thoughts of it, or of Burt, out of her mind. It was difficult, though. She slept with the light on for the next week, because the entity continued trying to enter her psychic space, as if responding to her cutting ties with Burt. This felt like a form of psychic attack, as if the entity within Burt was angry because it could no longer feed off of Francine through the emotionally draining love affair.

Burt then started posting public messages on his page that were indirect jibes and barbs about Francine. It seemed as if he were angry at her private, friends-only, message, although he never responded to her personally. A few days later, Burt removed the photo of the other woman he proclaimed to love, as if in an apology. He also posted some nice things about Francine, this time veiled in romantic prose.

Francine recalls, "I felt as if my emotions were being pulled back and forth like a ping pong ball. On the outside Burt seemed like such a neat guy, sexy, heartfelt, and spiritual. But in person he avoided eye contact, acted rejecting and I could not feel any affection coming from him, as if he were blank. Then, when the entity attacks started happening, I realized it must be connected in some strange way to Burt's unusual behavior and the way he seemed to have a sixth sense when calling or posting things. It was as if this invisible entity were feeding off my attention and emotions."

The sad thing about this is that both Francine and Burt both were actively seeking their soul mate and he even made this known on his online networking pages. "From now on," Francine said, "I'm sticking to maintaining much stronger boundaries, and won't be deceived by online profiles. It's clear that one has to be cautious in more ways than simple dating rules. Gut instinct is more trustworthy."

After several weeks of no contact with Burt, the visits by the invisible entity stopped, although Francine did dream of Burt from time to time.

*Max and Ishtar*

Max, an introspective, socially conscientious businessman from New Zealand, communicated with me for several years regarding my research with anomalous phenomena as well as spiritual warfare issues that manifest in interpersonal relationships. He had been working on a consciousness-raising social project when he met a woman named Ishtar. Max claimed that he had a premonition of Ishtar before he met her which detailed her exact characteristics. In his own words, Max recalled their first meeting, which felt as if it had been orchestrated by unseen forces.

"On the first date, in which I invited her to cook with me, the electricity in the house went dead. I phoned the power company, and they said the power shouldn't have been out, as all the other houses in the vicinity including neighbors had power. So we sat together with a candle going, and I felt as if we were being observed."

When Max related his feelings regarding the sense of being watched by something unseen, Ishtar told him that she felt his estranged ex-wife was interfering with her plans to be with him. Max, on the other hand, often felt that something was wrong and sensed he was fighting something unseen, especially after their breakup. He then started perceiving and referring to this invisible force as a third party entity.

During the span of the relationship, Max said that Ishtar would become emotionally manipulative and irrational. "Ishtar would often start arguments, after which I would go back to my place. After which she said she could feel my anguish and felt guilty about what she did. I always had this sense that she was never honest with me. She would appear to try and change the dynamics of the relationship and started treating me more like furniture, and then the relationship started to go downhill."

Max described Ishtar as if she had a strong alien presence controlling her thoughts and words, and on occasion he could hear her thoughts before she spoke them. Max said at that point in time, he had made some poor business and career decisions and found himself distracted from his own journey. He felt he was being directed away from his goals and instead became consumed with the drama that was unfolding around Ishtar. "At the same time," he said, "I found myself obsessing over her as she kept me on the edge, but I grew tired of chasing after her, as there was no recompense for the affection that I gave."

Max felt it made no sense that he had such strong feelings for Ishtar. He was confused why he should even have them at all; he saw no value in having any kind of relationship with her amid so much lying and deceit.

From the beginning, Max instinctively sensed something wrong with the relationship. Yet, he could not stop thinking about Ishtar and often "felt" her because the psychic bond was so close. He became physically affected and emotionally exhausted from being around her. After the breakup, he had physical sensations such as pain around the shoulders, as if something was draining energy from him. He believes he suffered soul damage, from a metaphysical perspective, with lots of pain in the throat region. During meditation and tapping into his intuitive inner body senses, Max sensed negative energy of a dark red and green color, as if it were channeled into his navel area, moving through his soul, and then back down to his lower back and out through his leg.

The breakup left him with physical symptoms of lower back pain, left leg calf muscle stiffness and pain in his throat. His blood pressure rose, as did his blood sugar, and he then developed depression from the emotional and psychological abuse.

In hindsight, Max believes Ishtar had a pathological lying problem from the beginning. She claimed to be empathetic and caring, yet at the same time she was very jealous and possessive, even stalking him in public. "She sent anonymous letters to me," he said, "and would stare at me from a downtown shop window when I was shopping, pretending not to see me, yet it was clear she was wanting to be seen."

The relationship only lasted eight months but it took Max a good seven years to heal. Even then, long after they broke up, he could still feel "her presence" as an invasive otherworldly entity.

*Lucy and Pepe*

Lucy, a thirty-nine year old mother of three, had recently separated from her emotionally unavailable husband. Lucy is also an alien-MILAB abductee,* and believes her own marriage had been manipulated by her alien handlers in such a way that chaos resulted. It was a long, unfulfilling marriage that became verbally and emotionally abusive towards the end, until finally she had enough. To lift her spirits, she decided to spend a weekend with girlfriends on a bus trip from Southern California to Laughlin, Nevada. She needed time away from her husband to sort out her thoughts and have some needed space from the dark cloud of their rocky, crumbling marriage.

Pepe, a single man in his thirties, had not planned to go on

---

* See Appendix for more on MILABS.

the Laughlin trip. Through a twist of fate, he was given his mother's bus ticket when she became ill at the last moment, and his sister did not want to go alone. He spotted Lucy and her girlfriends, chatting and giggling in a couple of seats several rows up and across from him. Lucy kept looking back at Pepe, because as she described it, "I could feel him staring at me as if he was reading my energy."

During that bus ride Lucy recalled a dream she had a few weeks earlier of being on that same bus, but in her dream the bus crashed and flipped over. She felt ill at ease because she remembered seeing a man exactly like Pepe in her dream. At one point in the drive, the bus seemed to swerve, but nothing happened and all was safe. No accident. Lucy and Pepe stole glances at each other a few times during the ride, and so Lucy decided to play some psychic games to see if Pepe was responsive to her telepathic signals. She would turn her face away from Pepe, pretending not to see him while saying in her mind, "Turn around, look at me."

Sure enough, Pepe turned around on cue a couple of times, as if he could hear her in his mind.

Midway to Laughlin, the bus tour stopped at a rest stop and convenience store so that the travelers could refresh themselves. Lucy decided to get off and walk towards the restrooms and said in her mind towards Pepe, "Follow us and go to the restroom area."

Pepe casually walked in the same direction, and after Lucy and her girlfriend walked out of the restroom they saw Pepe standing nearby watching them exit. Pepe and Lucy made eye contact and Lucy broke the ice, introduced herself and said, "Hello".

Pepe was receptive and happy to meet Lucy. They exchanged casual pleasantries and went to the store next door to buy a few snack items. At that moment Lucy said she felt a deja-vu of having met Pepe before, and experienced a distinct psychic connection, even though they didn't know each other

—yet. She wondered if Pepe could read her mind, as he seemed very perceptive to her mental signals.

While in Laughlin, Pepe and Lucy exchanged phone numbers, but that was all. Pepe promised to call, and did so about a month after the trip. He invited her to visit him at his home, about thirty miles away, and offered to take her out to dinner. After the date, Pepe kissed Lucy. She described it as a heightened kiss, the kind in storybooks. Lucy said, "Oh my God, I've never had that kind of kiss before. Sparks flew and we both wanted more."

But Lucy wanted to keep the relationship light for the time being, as the separation from her husband was still in progress and extremely stressful. They talked almost nightly on the phone, and visited a few times at Pepe's house.

After three months into the relationship, they could no longer resist the build-up and gave in to their desires. Lucy and Pepe shared a powerful connection. As Lucy put it, "the sex was amazing, so much so that I nearly had out of the body experiences while we made love. It was that good!"

One of the unusual things Lucy noticed about Pepe is that while they were having sex, Lucy could see another darkish entity overshadowing Pepe, as if it were partially in and out of his body. She only saw this ghostly entity when they were having sex. Lucy had conflicting thoughts of pleasure and guilt about sex with Pepe. It was as if he, or the entity within him, knew exactly what could arouse her to an unnatural degree, to the point that she experienced altered states of consciousness during sex. On several occasions Lucy thought she saw an entity with a lizard-like, gargoyle face. The entity's ghostly body was much larger than Pepe.

The two experienced a very strong empathetic connection to each other. Lucy could feel when Pepe was happy, sad, or yearning for her sexually, even at a distance and without verbally communicating. Pepe could tune into her the same way. Yet, even though their sex was highly arousing and orgasmic, their relationship started falling apart as Pepe became emotionally unstable displaying outbursts of anger and depressive mood swings.

Gargoyle image, from Wiki Commons

Soon after they started having sexual relations, Pepe became possessive and jealous. If Lucy wore a blouse or article of clothing that revealed too much skin, he told her to change, even though temperatures often climbed above 100 degrees and many people wore shorts and tank tops. His eyes were constantly darting around searching for evidence of other men looking her up and down, as if Lucy were "asking for it." Pepe started interrogating Lucy about what men she was seeing and what she was doing when he wasn't with her.

Lucy also began having more nightmares. Even when they were not together, she experienced what she called astral sexual visits by the entity that was somehow connected to Pepe. She wondered if the entity was in part responsible for Pepe's sudden jealousy, anger, and control issues.

They had an on and off relationship for nearly eight years, breaking up several times. During these break-ups, Lucy would casually date other men. Each time, Pepe became more jealous and even threatened violence against the other men. Pepe had an ability to manipulate Lucy with his sob stories, and because the sex was so good, Lucy forgave him and got back together with him.

But Pepe never changed. The last straw was reached when he threatened Lucy's last date, named Alejandro. Unknown to Lucy, Alejandro called his bluff, visited Pepe at his home, and saw him for what he was: a small, insecure man whose bark was louder than his bite. Intimidated and humiliated, Pepe backed off from Alejandro and continued to beseech Lucy's sympathies. Disgusted and embarrassed that Alejandro saw Pepe's true colors; Lucy broke it off with Pepe forever. After the tumultuous break up, Pepe told her he was going to commit suicide, hoping to win her over through pity, but it didn't work. In a last ditch effort to get back at Lucy, Pepe threatened her with, "If I can't have you then no one can!"

Lucy didn't take him seriously, and Pepe didn't follow through with his threats. By this time, Lucy and Alejandro were already an item. Lucy said that after that long, on-again off-again crazy, obsessive relationship, it didn't take long at all to heal. In fact, she was relieved when she finally broke it off completely with Pepe and has no regrets that she did so. "And", she added, "that dark, gargoyle-like entity no longer visited me or my dreams again."

*Maarit and Bjorn*

Maarit, a young Scandinavian housewife and mother, contacted me in response to my previous book, *The Love Bite*. Grateful to correspond with me concerning her anomalous life experiences relating to alien and military abductions, she had much to share about how she believed her marriage was supernaturally arranged. Or, as she put it, "orchestrated by the interdimensional beings who have been visiting me since childhood." In fact, Maarit had so many lucid memories regarding her alien and military abduction (MILAB) experiences, that I interviewed her for two articles that appeared on my web site[*] in April and December of 2011, and in the Italian magazine, *X-Times* in October of 2011. The first interview is in the Appendix for those who are interested in the alien abduction and MILAB testimonial, as well as comments on her relationship manipulations.

Many of the events in her life can make one truly wonder if advanced alien "watchers" had an influence in her life, much like what was portrayed in the 2011 movie, *The Adjustment Bureau*. In her own words, Maarit describes how she met Bjorn, her husband, and the unusual events that led to their union.

> "Before I met Bjorn, we both had previous relationships that had just ended. We both had a strong feeling to find someone despite the fact that we weren't looking for a permanent relationship. We actually met through a blind date and sensed *déjà vu* immediately. We both felt we knew each other. I later wondered why I felt so charmed even if he did not satisfy me intellectually. He was drawn to me and I couldn't get rid of him. I did feel that my reactions and decisions were made under a certain kind of psychological

---

[*] See http://evelorgen.com/wp/

mood out of the ordinary. I just acted, not reflected, like a robot. It was as if the two of us were mentally programmed to form a relationship and live together. We both were dependent on each other and didn't have family and our financial situation was not good. And looking back, I think there was nothing that either of us could have done to break this. We have been married for over seventeen years.

We also had some paranormal activity after we had decided to move together to Helsinki. I left my former post-graduate studies at the University of Tampere to be with him. We both heard odd noises in our home at night, as did others who stayed with us. Once a flower, that was originally placed in a bookshelf, was found as if set neatly in the middle of the floor when we came home. We both felt as if an alien presence was in the house one night, and that night we both woke up from a sleep state in which our consciousness was somehow melded as one. The experience was beyond description.

Other times, we just seemed to be in tune because when we both went to the grocery store without telling each other what we wanted to buy-we both ended up getting the same things. This happens all the time, we don't even have to speak."

When I asked Maarit if she experienced out-of-the-ordinary drama, chaos, or emotional draining during the relationship, she told me she had many doubts as to whether the relationship would last. But as it turned out, she had few options but to work issues out, as "The Adjustment Bureau Team" on their case exerted a heavy hand and made sure she and Bjorn stayed together for reasons about which we can only speculate.

She described in more detail:

"In the early parts of the marriage it was an emotional roller coaster. Bjorn became cold and reckless. He used alcohol and engaged in intense physical training. He produced lots of drama through

> **Many of the events in her life can make one truly wonder if advanced alien "watchers" had an influence in her life, much like what was portrayed in the 2011 movie, *The Adjustment Bureau*.**

his drinking patterns. When he had these cold and reckless episodes, his personality and even facial expression changed. During the alcohol-provoked episodes the whole room became so cold. It seemed he enjoyed causing me emotional suffering. I remember thinking that this was unreal somehow, and there were hidden aggressive intentions as well in his gestures and words.

    This took a lot of energy from me. His behavior seemed intense during the exact period of time when I was learning shiatsu massage, practicing meditation and yoga. Every time I felt spiritually connected, he dragged me down. It was difficult for me because at that time I was financially dependent and my career progression was obviously on hold. I didn't have anyone to go to, as my family is gone. Bjorn was controlling and very jealous, he wouldn't allow me to be reached by any male. He would verbally manipulate also, but I put a stop to this and revealed what his behavior patterns were doing to us. Every time I decided to leave him he changed his mode of behavior, into that of a small, neglected, abused boy seeking understanding.

    Now, reflecting back on those years I felt he was influenced or possessed by some evil force that was able to hide his true human empathy and reasoning side. I did an enormous job to bring him into the light of understanding, and we had many reflective discussions about this.

We have been healing our relationship and ourselves as long as we have been married. Now we have mutual respect, a strong and warm relationship and parenthood. We both see ourselves as a team.

Of course I have changed over the years, I am a fighter for justice and no one can emotionally walk over me and my respect for authorities is zero!"

Maarit and Bjorn represent a couple that prevailed against forces attempting to isolate her or orchestrate chaos around them. I believe Maarit's strength of character and perseverance to heal herself and her husband helped defend against Cupid's dark side. In their situation, it took an immense effort, primarily on her part, to stand firmly in her truth, despite the odds.

For more information on Maarit's alien abductions please go to Appendix for an in-depth interview.

Chapter 8

# Category Four: Psychic Vampirism, Psychopathic Partners, and Paranormal Activity

The last category of stories from the Dark Side of Cupid represent more severe cases of psychic vampirism, where one partner is believed to be heavily overshadowed by a third party entity. This entity is suspected to be the culprit behind the manifestations of psychic vampirism, paranormal activity, and psychopathic behaviors in the psychic vampire partner. These persons also believe their relationship to have been supernaturally arranged and influenced throughout the entire duration of their love affair. Physical complaints such as solar plexus sensations and exhaustion are characteristic of psychic vampirism, as opposed to simple emotional vampirism.

*Amy and Thomas*

Amy met Thomas, a successful chiropractor, while she went in for a spinal adjustment in the city where she worked. For the sake of convenience, she often tried to set appointments during her lunch hour or right after work. Amy recalled, "When I first met the Doctor, initially I had no interest in him. Shortly thereafter, I became enamored of him, and then became obsessed with him. This seemed to happen innocently enough, with my offer of friendship."

But Amy soon picked up on a strong psychic connection with this man, and she felt powerful sexual energies being activated in her after the chiropractic adjustments. This had never happened to her before. Amy, having the second sight, felt as if Thomas was also psychic because she experienced what she called "astral visits" from the doctor. Not just that, but the doctor exuded a strong presence, a sexy charisma that

Mephistopheles, from Wikicommons

swept Amy off her feet. This combination caused her to become yet more obsessed. Amy even decided to join the same religious spiritual path as the doctor, Judaism.

As Amy explored her spiritual path alongside the doctor, she noticed a heightened degree of psychic sensitivity, and saw spirits, such as tall robed Nordics and an unpleasant troll spirit. She told me that this troll spirit looked very similar to a drawing she saw in an old book on King Solomon of Mephistopheles.

She also experienced increasing sexual energies emanating from Thomas, especially while he was giving her chiropractic adjustments. Amy candidly admitted, "It was only after I received chiropractic adjustments from the "good Doctor" that

I first started experiencing very startling strong waves of sexual energy from him. I realized that he was on his own orchestrating these energies, and I even saw him do a type of energy extraction from me. He seemed to use the solar plexus area to draw and absorb energies from me, which were extremely sensual and ecstatic at the same time."

Amy was mystified and yet enjoyed the sensual energies that the doctor seemed to send to her and elicit out of her. Although the doctor was married, they began an affair, consummating their strong connection with many secret rendezvous full of passionate sex. Amy describes, "While I was with the doctor, or rather when I first became under his spell, I could not eat very much and had trouble sleeping. For years since, I still wake up in the middle of the night without fail. I call this the 'witching hour,' for it was primarily during these times that the Doctor cast his spell of lust over me, and I would be caught up in the throes of ecstatic tantric bliss, gasping and writhing upon the bed for hours."

I asked Amy why she thought the doctor put a spell over her. She described to me in more detail the various ghostly presences and spirits that visited her only after becoming involved with the Doctor and his religion.

"Many spirits came to lead me further on that spiritual path. They watched over me, and seemed to monitor my progress in that religion. There were Nordic spirits in biblical-looking robes who not only upheld the connection between the Doctor and me, but they blessed our union which really had the effect of keeping me imprisoned, as it were, in the obsessive relationship."

On several occasions, Amy saw the familiar spirit that she associated with the Doctor. A familiar spirit is one that is connected to another individual, who serves them. This occurs in some forms of witchcraft, where a specific spirit or demon is invoked and assigned to serve the witch or magician.

Amy explained, "At first, when I was totally under the

Doctor's spell, I saw this spirit lots of times, but I just ignored it or did not give it any credence. I saw a very short, dwarfed and odd shaped spirit, very dark in color with a large, bumpy, misshapen head. A type of troll spirit. Believe it or not, I have actually seen pictures of this same spirit after I saw it, which led me to believe that it is a demonic force, which has been used before by others in occult circles for advancement in the material world. This spirit has been with the Doctor for many years and is still with him to date."

I asked Amy to describe this troll spirit in more detail, and she said, "It had a big pot-belly, his legs were shorter than his upper torso and he had these very large and ugly feet with long talons. His rather large head was bumpy and came to a point. The coloration was dark, though – black-as-sin, like Mephistopheles."

Their affair lasted for more than ten years. Amy's love obsession with him led her to extend the relationship long after she would have, had she been in her right mind. But she was adamant that the good Doctor – as she called him – had an occult psychic stronghold over her, even inducing sexual sensations from a distance. If you recall, this was also noted by another Dark Side of Cupid client, Anna, who called it telesthesia. Amy described these tantric, ecstatic throes of sexual energies as if the doctor's spirit astrally visited her - usually during the witching hour.

"During our lengthy entanglement of ten-plus years I experienced psychic sensitivity and growth on a parallel that I never knew existed. For example, I could see through his eyes and even feel the same feelings and emotions that he was feeling, a real empathic connection. Of course, most of the time it was surrounding or involved with lust. For example, I could see in my minds eye, Thomas, as he looked through a magazine with a scantily clad, sexy woman with nude buttocks protruding. I felt his feelings and immediately more lustful and tantric feelings assailed me, as if I were inside of him. We felt as if we shared the same body at times."

When asked if the Doctor had a love obsession with her, Amy responded that his obsession was always over sex, not love. In fact, Amy now believes he was a sex addict, and he even had an affair with her best friend behind her back. Amy, like many other women who have dated married men, hoped he would leave his wife. But the doctor used his marriage and family life to hide behind, so he could avoid making any kind of serious commitment to Amy. She was in love with him, but he was not in love with her.

Amy battled the inner voice inside of her, which told her the doctor was a dangerous man. Every time Amy tapped into Thomas psychically, she felt high, as if on drugs. Amy recalled, "His spirit seemed to invade my very being, and it seemed that I had found the magic elixir of life! I could do no wrong, make no mistakes, everything I touched turned golden. Whenever I was between jobs and in need of money, he had the power to bring me money via jobs. Something always came in magically whenever he said it would."

But crashing emotional lows always followed sooner or later. After one passionate liaison with the Doctor, Amy decided to call him later at work, just to say hello because, she told me, "I felt his energies so strongly that day. After one really good love making session with the Doctor, feeling that he was also thinking of me lovingly and wanting to hear the sound of my voice, I called his office just to say hi. It's usual to do these types of things with a loved one. I've done this before with other boyfriends. However, his reception of my phone call was so cold and abrupt, my little heart was shattered. I felt utterly confused, crushed and broken-hearted. Then he called me back a few days later, wanting his usual booty call."

The Doctor's booty calls continued for a while, until Amy discovered he was pursuing her best friend. Once Amy realized this, she made efforts to break it off with him. But oddly enough, Amy remarked, "when I was endeavoring to extricate myself from him entirely, this is when he found it easy to pop up at my apartment in the wee hours of the morning seeking sex. I turned him away, though. Of course this showed me that he could have spent more quality time with me had he really wanted to. It was easy for him to shadow me and pop up unexpectedly when he felt his grasp over me loosening. He preferred to keep our liaisons scheduled for his secret lunch breaks every day. Thereafter he would shower, and return to his practice, happy, whistling, renewed, and invigorated while I was left drained, saddened and used up. That bastard!"

Amy found it difficult to break up with Thomas because of his powerful domination over her emotionally and sexually. She tried to break up several times, but always came back to him, like an addiction.

"Our affair progressed even stronger, and I felt strangled by his refusal to leave his wife and family, and his insistence that we just 'stay the same.' I was determined to see other men. During one such occasion of seeing another man, the doctor showed up at my apartment unannounced, right after the new boyfriend left. When the Doctor showed up unannounced I told him that he shouldn't be there and that I now had a boyfriend, to which he responded, 'oh well of course you can have other friends, but I come first.' At that point I knew he had gone off the tracks and after forcing him to leave, I determined that the relationship with him was permanently over."

She knew it was going to kill her unless she broke all ties with the doctor forever.

"When I tried to break if off with the Doctor," Amy explained, "he would not accept this action. I felt trapped and was in a lot of emotional pain. I really loved him and felt that he was a part of my soul, but I knew inside that it was over. To relieve the pain and anguish I felt, I drank heavily and smoked marijuana each day for two weeks, which was not usual for me at all."

Chapter 8: Case Files, Category Four

To add insult to injury, Amy discovered that Thomas had offered her best friend money, when Amy was now financially destitute. He flaunted it, knowing full well that she was out of work. What he did not know was that Amy had become pregnant. She miscarried, however, and never said a word about it. Months later, Amy found the resolve to confront the Doctor on the phone about his affair with her best friend. He denied it until she came to his office in person and confronted him there. Finally, he admitted it, and then had the audacity to attempt to rescue and revive their affair.

"It was useless on his part," said Amy. "The affair was over, finally over and I was now free to really live my life without his overriding, overwhelming control and dominance. It was the dawn of a new day! I have never gone back to him, but I often do look back in sorrow and regret."

Even though Amy has much regret over the affair with the Doctor, she has learned to bounce back with humor and remarkable resilience. Her second sight has aided her in vindicating the things she sensed about the Doctor, and many other things. Whenever she sees the familiar troll spirit and other demons associated with the Doctor, she commands them to leave. I had to laugh when she called them "The Butt Uglies"! Does Cupid employ an army of trolls?

*Wiz and Koral*

Wiz, a South American artist and musician in his late 30's, met Koral, a young, svelte, mystifying seductress while on tour in Bogotá, South America. In Wiz's own words he described their magical first meeting.

> "I met Koral as we – a group of artists and musicians – were invited to Bogotá to begin a creative musical project for an important festival. On our first debut, with the purpose of celebrating opening night, we ventured off into the colonial old town next to our hotel. There in the festive air we came upon a small

quaint café where the sign in Spanish read, 'De Pelicula,' translated 'Out of the Movies.'

"Inside the café was glass pane blue. Archways, wine racks and amber candles, it was like a cinema boutique. We boastfully positioned ourselves at a small door-style table exhibiting our own exotic qualities. And then, She happened.

"At first she was like a strange androgynous young girl. She was intense and intriguing. Doing the catwalk. Admittedly, I was an easy lure, all pretentious and horny. Still she was just so fascinating; I could swear her face went in and out of focus, like a blurry hologram. All at once it came over me; "Oh my God it's her! The eyes of Frida Kahlo. It's her – my virtual muse." She fixed her glare on mine. I entered passion...and Chaos.

"She was dark, dense and fascinating. Such a seductive enigma like a beautiful, venomous, wild orchid. However, curiously, whenever I was most sane,

*The Vampire* (1897) by Phillipe Burne-Jones. From Wiki Commons.

> I could see she was actually quite plain. During our choreographed courtship, in her small makeshift room, there was a movie poster with her very image, yet it was another actress...absolutely striking. The character's name rhymed with arrachnea."

Wiz went on to tell me that after his initial magical meeting with Koral, they met for a full week of wonder and fantasy, as if in the thrill of a tease, until the last night of his visit in the foreign city. Wiz says,

"It wasn't until the last night in that foreign city that she came for me. Till then every encounter was a thrill and a tease, but that night I found myself in an otherworldly trance, mesmerized, hypnotized. She hovered over my pelvis, winding her thighs, swaying her arms. I was paralyzed into impotent awe."

Wiz explained in disbelief that he sensed a snakelike shape metamorphizing out of her mouth:

"With her head cocked back, it was dancing like an arm over my naked vulnerable being. This was delirious. Unbelievable but all too real. The snake-like limb slashed down, snagging the area over my navel, surging into the solar plexus. I was in utter shock and inevitably lost consciousness."

Wiz admitted to having a horrible hangover, but this was more serious. Unreal.

"The next morning I discovered her leaving the shower and rushing to work, and so we bade a quick farewell. During the trip home, my solar plexus area became increasingly uncomfortable and my mind was inundated with flashes of her. My memories seemed vague, while relentlessly the discomfort had transformed into a twisting contorting knot.

Abruptly after returning home, in a waking state I perceived this "knot" erupt with hundreds if not thousands of tiny opaque transparent spider like creatures which swiftly dispersed over my body and being, spinning an etheric web around and of my very soul. I heaved in thrushes of pain, entering a state of ecstatic shock."

After this experience Wiz had the impulse to hear Koral's voice, and so he lifted the phone to call, and yet received no dial tone. Only silence. Then to Wiz's amazement at that very moment, he heard her utter the words, "Hello?"

Wiz was love bitten and a few months passed with flights to and from Bogotá. He entered that same café, proud of his courage to be meeting Koral again, but she behaved as if unimpressed. They came together for days at a time for grinding sex and emotional taunting until Koral asked Wiz to leave. Wiz described going through several weeks of a lonely period of chronic hunger, desperation, lucid dreaming, and out of the body experiences. He toured a few cities in a show called Insomnia with the logo of a snake eye, then returned to visit Koral triumphantly.

This time, Wiz said, "Koral was pleased. Almost immediately she moved in with me. From then on, perpetual sabotage. Koral could talk for hours, she would stare forever...And so, given to and driven by alcohol, tobacco and caffeine use, she practiced nightly sleep deprivation, constant teasing and sexual milking of me; I would be her apprentice."

I asked Wiz to tell me about any emotional manipulation or more unusual behaviors about Koral. He told me,

"When I held back my emotional involvement with her, she would go into a wild array of attitudes...needy, then evasive, teasing for affection, and then chastising. It was enough to drive you mad. There was always some serious dispute over anything I deemed important; she or something through her was toying and feeding on my thought waves and vital energy. The more I centered on knowledge, independence, and self-preservation, the more irrational and erratic she would become."

Wiz commented that there were times before Koral abandoned him that she would suddenly appear out of nowhere, simply after the thought of her. He recalled one particularly lucid memory:

"Especially one day when she appeared like a withered flower and I beheld her flush, from grayish and pale, back into color with my very presence while the knot in my solar plexus twisted inward."

She also trained him in the Tao of Chi and tantric sex.

"Sometimes she would urinate during my orgasms…was this some kind of courtesan's spermicidal technique, or a personal fetish? A Master of I Ching and only twenty-one! The way she saw, the things she said, she simply knew too much. But how?"

Wiz delved into Koral's dark, mysterious past, and found a closet of skeletons.

"She was a poor, only child, with no formal education except for standard primary and military high school. She was raised by a single mother, hippy and freestyle, who got pregnant by a young Spaniard traveler in a rigid Catholic society. In turn, her own mother demanded she and the Spaniard wed, which forced the young man on his way, leaving the mother-to-be grieving and ostracized. The unwanted little girl was then raised by the grandmother, a lower middle-class old widow with a simple downtown shoe store. She did not have a happy childhood."

Wiz sighed with a regretful pity, "I saw the images before they burned. One day the little girl, now late teens, happened by her mother across a city lane. The mother was all woe and derelict, the little girl arrogant, simply ignored her and walked on by. News came later; the sad young woman died a drug prostitute in a popular slum alley. A few years more and the grandmother corroded of cancer in the "little" girl's arms. Anguished and ostracized by her relatives, Koral fled into the wilderness and lived horseback in a remote cabin for a short while. Sometimes she would drift back to those moments in an attitude of inner discovery and adventure, one understood something "special" happened there. Then she returned to the big city. By 19, she'd aborted, snorted, and connived her way through certain circles of the intellectual Bohemian city maze. As a dark object of desire, she evoked alternating emotions in different people; suspicion, lust, admiration, envy, compassion."

Wiz continued in his bittersweet reveries,

"Impulsively, compulsively, she scribbled, undulated and exorcised in automatic writing, with never ending diaries, any paper will do – all fragmented prose, her texts a bazaar of torment, flower clippings, samples of wisdom and lost forgotten mythologies, emotional fencing, a play of mirrors, and beautiful literary brilliance... or was it perhaps profound schizophrenia? Her voice was a mimic of a prude radio personality who conducted a classical music show, which was transmitted each morning. Like a spontaneous lunatic, immediately after playing a spoiled naughty Lolita, she was a new age gypsy diva, only to later unleash a hysterical, vibrant shrew."

Wiz recalled how he felt during this dark time in graphic finesse, "Tied to her entrails, I allowed my Self to fall into wretched misery. I was gifted with a penthouse place, but soon after she moved in, the administration made complaints. My attitude polarized to that of her self-declared protector and with excessive pride, we desperately sought out an alternate abode. I was exhausted and under such pressure, we decided to move to the first small cheap suite that appeared. It was terrible.

During this dark space, one of her sketches revealed her lurid vision of my soul probing from a cocoon. The cocoon was settled in an ephemeral flower, colored like a bruised fuchsia. I understood this image as my escapades to the astral place to replenish my spoiled reserves. I had succumbed to an anorexic state of quasi-existence. She would be drunk, dreamy and glowy with my own scarce energy. I was hell. From the deep bowels of my being, the worst surged, we both breathed shit, wired on pleasure, hopeless lovers, like flaccid junkies. She was fierce. I was bled of will and cried for light. *The Bardo Thodol, The Book of the Dead*, I delved into the shelves of the city library, seeking refuge, seeking Truth."

With flair, Wiz described his final days with Koral, as if a choreographed mythical drama was determined to have the last play on words:

"During this inferno, she gave me Dante's book, his songs so describe this Divine Riddle. Read HELL. First song. Seventeenth song. Twenty-fourth song. From within and without this cosmic cocoon, I understood my Self as an omphalus, vesica pisces, the luminous egg of energy we emanate. This ova was encoiled by a serpentine being, as I rediscovered my Self to Be…the Divine Seed, this viper's precious treasure."

I reeled in amazement at the diabolical drama that unleashed its web of endless riddles and mockery in Wiz's life. If there ever was a Dark Side of Cupid, this was it.[*]

*Michelle and Bernie, the Reverend*

Michelle, an active, seasoned woman in the teaching profession, began dating a Reverend named Bernie, who visited from out of town. She told me she wasn't particularly attracted to him physically, but at the same time was compelled to maintain a friendship, since Bernie was involved in many charitable social activities with various volunteer organizations.

Michelle admitted that shortly after meeting Bernie, they had sex, which was out of character for her. She explained, "That first night was a magical experience. It felt wonderful! I felt immense passion and sex drive for this man like I've never experienced in my entire life. However, when I look back, and due to my older age, I realized this relationship was

---

[*] Reprinted with permissions, excerpts from "The Viper's Enchantment" by Wiz Kinnigin
http://www.kininigin.com/VIPER%20STORY%20I.htm

only sexual."

It wasn't long before Michelle started noticing paranormal activity after meeting Bernie. A month or two into the relationship, Michelle felt ghostly presences around the Reverend, whom she thought might be his two ex-wives giving her their "approval" of some sort from beyond the grave to be with this man.

But after being with him six months and during a four-week absence from Bernie, she "was attacked by an invisible force." According to Michelle:

"These were frightening, physical, yet invisible attacks, which occurred during different hours of the morning, sometimes for two hours at a time. I had trouble getting any rest during that month. I finally realized that these attacks were related to my partner, whom I knew could somehow connect with me energetically from a distance, as he had done this other times before. So I reached out to him, but he denied he knew anything about it."

Michelle later had a chance to confront the Reverend: "That's when I realized he was actually connected to a spirit or entity of some sort, and that entity then – through my partner – openly showed me how he could control me mentally and restrain me physically with seemingly no effort."

Despite the alarming incongruence with the Reverends normal appearance and his unusual behaviors and his show of control over Michelle, she still was obsessed with him for at least six months. This was not characteristic of Michelle at all.

"I was obsessed to have sex with him, to be with him in person and to talk with him by phone for hours at a time. I let so much in my life go by the wayside because of this relationship, which turned out to be disastrous for my physical health, emotional health, finances and work reputation."

Michelle told me that the entire nine-month relationship was emotionally draining to say the least.

"Two months after we met, my immune system took a dive

*Chapter 8: Case Files, Category Four*

after a surgery. The surgery should have been fairly simple. However, I've been continuously ill with something or the other ever since then. It's now been over a year since I first met the Reverend, and I'm still struggling with fatigue and a lowered immune system."

When looking back, Michelle admitted she did things out of character for her when getting involved with the Reverend.

"I had sex shortly after we met – with someone who I wasn't attracted to. I did not use protection, like a condom, and I put my physical and emotional health, work reputation, and finances in serious jeopardy over this relationship."

Michelle said there were times after having been together daily with lots of sex for a week or more, that he would disappear for days or weeks at a time as if he was "turned off," which she could not understand.

When asked if Michelle thought her partner was emotionally manipulative, she relayed this, "Yes, he emotionally manipulated me, such as through jealous accusations, his condescending attitude toward my attempt at prayers at mealtime, how I spent my own money and my unwillingness to believe as he did religiously about homosexuality. He tried to make me feel shameful and unworthy of him because I divorced over twenty years ago and said he would never normally date anyone who was ever divorced."

Michelle said the Reverend was also generally controlling of her, which escalated over time.

"I could talk to this man in a frank, direct manner outside of sex. During sexual relations, though, he was overtly demanding, controlling and aggressive with me. Whenever we had sex, he essentially raped me and was so rough I often had bruises. That was painful to me, and I would beg him to please stop and never do that again. But, I could never stop or refuse this man from anything he wanted to do that was sexual in nature."

Michelle was traumatized over the strangeness of this

situation, as she had never dated a man like this with such "hypnotic control" over her when he touched her in certain ways and during sexual activity. When asked whether Michelle thought the Reverend might be possibly psychopathic in nature or perhaps harbored a non-human entity or a demon she said,

"Yes, I believe my former partner is psychopathic in nature. He is intelligent, appears very normal and has fairly close extensive ties with his family and community. However, he is not capable of the emotions of love or empathy. He is extremely controlling with only one emotion of occasional anger. I mean, he can laugh and be amused, but his range of emotions outside of anger is extremely limited."

Michelle observed the Reverend's interpersonal behaviors like this:

"He appears to work from an internal script about how he should project his feelings to others – of what is acceptable and appropriate. For a number of reasons, I believe this man may be part reptilian. He talked regularly about "Master" in both the third and first person. I believe he is controlled by something else – a parasitic reptilian from outside our dimension, which I fully realize sounds crazy."

What she didn't know is that I have heard this several times from others with very similar "love bite" relationship dynamics. Could Cupid have scales like a lizard? Or does Cupid employ reptilian middlemen?

Michelle said that even though the relationship only lasted nine months, and she had just ended it about a month prior to our interview, she is still cautious and concerned that the Reverend will try to come back into her life. She stated, "I believe he brought an unholy entity into my life, which may still be with me but seems to be weaker now, as I am still trying to heal from this relationship."      Even though Michelle broke off communication with Bernie, the lizard-like, invasive entity kept returning. She had several nightmares of various figures trying to re-assert control with threatening

## Chapter 8: Case Files, Category Four

Ancient Sumerian Reptilian entity.

comments, which often accompanied sexual aggression. Michelle tried various shamanic methods of healing and entity detachment, as well as hypnosis, in an attempt to reconnect to her inner soul power. This entity was quite persistent and the investigation is ongoing.

Healing is crucial, as I will discuss later, as well as self-empowerment and maintaining firm boundaries with these types of people.

### Gwen and Count Rokula

Gwen, a middle-aged divorced woman in a rural area of the Appalachian Mountains, has had alien abductions with military involvement (MILABs) since childhood. She has had numerous paranormal experiences in addition to the UFO and alien encounters, and believes her relationship interference to be directly related to her alien handlers or perhaps the military colluding with them. The aliens in her encounters are usually tall Greys, reptilians, military, and other assorted species, some quite malevolent.

Gwen had a difficult, long term marriage that took a turn for the strange in 1991, when her husband began a business partnership with a militant and secretive ex-Marine Corps friend. While he and his friend were away for the weekend, Gwen was delighted to have some personal space. On the day after her husband left for a four-day business trip, Gwen had a powerful vision of a man's face appear in her mind's eye. He had distinct and detailed features, but a haunting, evil laugh that frightened her. She tried to shake the vision, but it persisted in front of her face, as if it were a deliberate sent message from someone she would meet later in life.

After the vision, Gwen recalled that the night before, she dreamed of alien looking beings asking her questions about her current marriage, which was not going well. Gwen remembered asking for a new lover and for something new, not like her current husband or marriage situation. The alien beings asked for something in exchange, but the following day, Gwen could not recall what that was. At the time in the dream visit, she believed in the bargain she made with the alien beings. Little did she know that she made a deal with such a dark force that it would turn her life upside down and require years to put it all back together. In retrospect, she believes the man in her vision may have been the face of the devil himself – or at least someone like him.

Gwen met Count Rokula online through a Myspace connection, but not until 2005, fourteen years after that dream. He presented himself as an angel and spiritual healer. In fact, he called himself an Apostle, a preacher of the gospel. His emails were persistent and the connection between them was strong right from the beginning. They spent countless hours chatting online and on the phone. Rokula admitted to waiting for hours, watching diligently each day to see when Gwen came online to the list group they both chatted on. They communicated seven to eight months online and by telephone before they actually met in person. At the time, Gwen had not yet split up with her husband, but Rokula insisted she do so and even tried some magic to speed up the process. It turned out that during the same period that Gwen met Rokula online, her husband Dick started an affair with another woman.

From the moment Gwen and Rokula met in person, they were glued together. Gwen recalls:

"We thought it was a match made in heaven. He told me that he was sorry he didn't get here sooner and 'finally come home to him, that is,' as we both were convinced that we were designed for each other. We thought we knew and loved each other in past lives and had been forever looking to find each other destined for our reunion."

Rokula made statements to Gwen like, "I've been searching for you for a millennium. I'm so sorry it took so long to meet you."

He made overtures of religious fervor towards Gwen with grandiose phrases like, "I will heal thee. Now that you are here, I'm going to heal you."

Gwen reminisced that her meeting with Rokula in the beginning was like answered prayer. She thought he was her soul mate; their connection was so strong. Everything was perfect because at the same time she was going through a divorce, feeling lonely and anxious, Rokula appeared at the right time, rescuing her like a white knight in shining armor. He really rolled out the red carpet, and said things like "You are my goddess, my premium, God's gift to me."

When asked if this relationship felt orchestrated from the beyond Gwen and Rokula agreed that it was "definitely so."

Gwen said, "The feelings were not compared to any emotion experienced on this planet. It was beyond beautiful. We would go to the ends of the earth to be near each other."

In the beginning of the relationship with Rokula, everything was new, adventurous, and full of fun and excitement. They shared things between them fifty-fifty. They were in sync. The two lovers were on cloud nine and excitedly anticipated each other's company to the point they felt like they would die for one another. Gwen remarked, "We felt like we had been reunited from another life, another time, and had always known each other from previous lives and experiences. We were speaking each other's thoughts before the other would say anything. We were always connected. At the same time, it was like a grey fog hovering over the relationship. Every moment seemed like an exhausting eternity but yet there was such a strong uncontrollable desire to be with him that when it was time for us to part, I felt time had cheated us."

During their times apart, Gwen and her new lover talked on the phone for hours. Rokula called her several times a day and kept her on the phone sometimes for six or more hours a day, leaving her drained. Gwen gave me more details about how fatigued she got when in Rokula's presence:

"He claimed he had to be just near me or hearing my voice because it kept him alive and energized. When we were together he would smother my space. He would talk so much, my head would hurt and I just felt so tired and drained in his company. He would leave me feeling so weak sometimes I would spend several days in my pajamas. My stomach would always hurt in his presence and I never had stomach problems like that before I met him."

It got to the point that Gwen would consume more food, drink and vitamins before his arrival so she would have enough energy to deal with him. Even though Gwen felt exhausted after being with Rokula, she admitted, "His embrace was always desirable, yet extremely draining. When we were together I remember always wondering where the time went. The energy would just be zapped from my body like a long-term illness when lying on a hospital bed."

Gwen started to see all the masks Rokula wore. He made many grandiose claims, especially in his religious preaching mode in public. He often challenged Christians about certain scriptures and got into heated arguments with them, ultimately proving himself right and them wrong. One face was a preacher, apostle, and charismatic healer. Then there was the rock and roll god. Apparently, no one could play the guitar like Count Rokula! He claimed that he blew Carlos Santana away. Jimmy Hendrix? Well, he made Hendrix sound like a kindergartner pulling plastic toy strings! During his music gigs, he told the starry-eyed female groupies that he could use his fingers orgiastically on them as well as he could on the guitar.

Oddly enough, Gwen noticed a heightened degree of psychic sensitivity when with Rokula. She also said there was an increase in paranormal activity and ghostly presences during the three-year trauma-drama relationship. One night, Gwen had a very terrifying dream she believed to be a visitation of an evil entity that called himself Satan. It happened one night as she and Rokula lay sleeping together in the home she owned for twenty-five years. In her own words she stated:

"Rokula and I were asleep one night and I had a dream that seemed so real. A strange fog and bright light following it was trying to move through the bottom of the doors in my bedroom and in the dream I got up and was trying to escape, so I ran into the bathroom and shut the door. The fog and light was then moving under that door and came inside. So, in the dream I ran into the master bedroom and hurriedly dashed over to the dresser where a Bible was. I took the Bible and ran back into the bathroom where the fog and light had then found its way through the door and was forming a figure, which then turned into a naked man. He stood there and he laughed at me with his foot propped up against the bathtub and he said, "Do you think that Bible is going to save you Gwen? Don't you realize that there is nothing in that Bible that I don't understand? I know every word of it and it won't save you." Then he said, "I AM SATAN."

The dream was so real and I just felt trapped, afraid and angry. So, for whatever reason, I reached up and put my hands around Satan's throat and he was trying to take me while I was choking him. I woke up beside Rokula, terrified.

What was even more alarming was that Rokula also had a very similar dream.

"At the same moment," Gwen continued, "Rokula woke up and we just lay there for a few minutes looking at each other. I could see a strange fear in his eyes and I know he saw it in mine because before I said anything about what I had dreamed about, he spoke.

"Rokula began to tell me that he had awakened from a really bad dream. I said nothing about my nightmare and he continued with his. He told me that in the dream he was angry with me and that before he woke up he was leaning over my dead body trying to bring me back to life. I asked him why? Then what he told me scared the hell out of me. This is what he said, 'I was trying to bring you back to life because I had choked you to death in my dream.'"

Gwen recalls, "I could sense something, a presence very, very evil in that room with us when we woke up."

Gwen remarked on the switch of persons in the dream. "So in my dream I was choking Satan and in Rokula's dream he was choking me."

Even though Gwen had lived in that house for over two decades, she had never in her life ever felt or experienced anything like that before.

"The air was so cold and you could feel such evil. Rokula and I got up because we both refused to go back to sleep and the air was just different. We walked out into the hallway that leads downstairs and commented that we both felt something following us. Something evil was there but we couldn't see it. We came downstairs and right before the entry to my kitchen in a specific spot we could feel something, a presence so cold that we both started shivering like we were standing in a freezer."

On another occasion they experienced a mutually shared dream that turned out to be a life-threatening premonition, years later. They both dreamed of a bad car accident that Gwen had. At that time, it was simply a scary dream but it wasn't until January of 2010 that the dream would come true.

By six months into the passionate love affair Gwen consistently started feeling emotionally drained by Rokula. It was as if he literally fed off of Gwen's life force and emotional output. They would spend two to four days together several times a month and Gwen recalled that each time they were together, she'd feel so drained in his presence that she had to take four to six hour naps after being with him. When he went back to his hometown several hours away, and when he was not around, Gwen's energy levels returned to normal. From then on Gwen started noticing Rokula's strange behaviors. The creepy thing about him was his fascination with her menstrual cycles. He was obsessed with her menstrual blood.

Rokula exhibited a strong charisma and persuasiveness with people and now with her. Gwen was a Christian with interests in the paranormal, but when discussing many of her experiences with Rokula, he tried to tell her she was wrong and essentially tried to program her by making her watch videos and listen to CDs, sometimes all night, that favored an atheist viewpoint.

Lord Vampire, from Wiki Commons

Even though Rokula cast himself as a healer and minister, he aimed to change Gwen's ideas about God. He also put on an air that he was an intelligent wealthy man, but as Gwen put it, after visiting his place several hours away, "He lived like a cockroach!"

He seemed to have many followers online who believed his charade of benevolent healer/minister but as time went on Gwen was starting to see through his many masks. But she was still in love with him. She did not want to believe he could be that bad.

In the beginning of the affair, Rokula placed her on a pedestal and showered her with attentiveness and romantic gestures by telling her that she was his "premium." Within a year's time, however, he was calling her "a dirty little peasant." He played her emotions like a yo-yo, one moment casting her in a highly cherished light, and in the next trampling on her emotionally as if she were a dirty, homeless, dog bitch. In Gwen's own words, "I went from being a premium to a child of a lesser God in his eyes. Emotionally, I was a yo-yo on a string. Up and down. I went from being a goddess to a dirty little peasant."

Still, after a year of being together, Rokula asked Gwen to marry him. Within a few months after the proposal, Gwen developed doubts about Rokula's sincerity and broke up with him. But Rokula had a way of making up, showering her with flowers and sweet talk. Before Gwen knew it, they were back together.

Count Rokula didn't change at all. He resumed his crazy-making behaviors, emotional abuse, and energy drains on Gwen. Not only this, but Gwen noticed something extremely disturbing about Rokula's home; an old, multi-story, dilapi-

> "I suppose that I should have listened to the red flags I had as early as 1991, when Rokula's face appeared to me, and when I heard his evil, sick laugh."

dated mansion with a secret basement he called the dungeon, with a sign on the door saying, "KEEP OUT." So one day, when Rokula disappeared for a short while, Gwen opened the basement door. There were several rooms, leading to more rooms. One was a small soundproof room that Rokula claimed was for music. But it was so small it could barely hold one person and no room for speakers. Another locked room was a makeshift, bedroom for his schizoid, depressive brother who was rarely seen or talked to anyone. In fact, Rockula kept his brother imprisoned there like a mentally ill subhuman, restricted from the upstairs home. Inside the dungeon bedroom was an entire wall organized with weapons like swords, sticks, chains, baseball bats, knives, and guns. Directly behind that was a long silver table that appeared to be the bed where he slept and on it were several hand cuffs, some of them with spikes and sexual toys nearby like dildos. Scary looking stuff.

"I suppose that I should have listened to the red flags I had as early as 1991, when Rokula's face appeared to me, and when I heard his evil, sick laugh. But as it turned out, the last straw on the camel's back happened when Rokula took me out to dinner for my birthday. Now, Rokula had the habit of talking to just about anyone he'd meet up with publicly, making boastful statements to pretty women such as, 'You're such a beautiful woman. I hope your husband or boyfriend is nice to you because if he isn't, I'll kick his ass.' He'd make pompous statements about being a preacher, powerful healer and that kind of thing."

So as Rokula and Gwen entered the restaurant for her birthday dinner, Rokula saw a morbidly obese woman, about 300 pounds, walking with her daughter into the waiting area as they also waited for a table. Rokula made a private comment to Gwen about the obese woman's smell and how disgusting she was, but in the next moment, he started up a conversation with the woman about his recent paranormal and conspiracy research. He was so involved with the conversation he decided to share a table with the obese woman, while leaving Gwen and the other woman's ten-year old daughter at another table. By this time Gwen, fuming with exasperation, didn't want to share a table with him but hoped he'd come back soon and have a private dinner with her. But Rokula stayed and talked with the obese woman for over three hours while Gwen and the confused daughter sat and ate at an adjacent table alone. All the while, Rokula mouthed off crazy talk with the fat woman, who certainly enjoyed the male attention she was getting. Rokula didn't leave her until he got her phone number, handwritten herself on a matchbook cover. Well, the fat lady didn't sing, but for Gwen it was over.

Gwen raced home that night and cried for hours. She told Rokula how deeply hurt she was, not to mention her humiliation and fury from being so rudely ignored on her birthday, as if her birthday meant nothing to him at all. And he would rather be with this other woman? What was wrong with him? Rokula had complete disregard for her feelings. Gwen recalled that this was one of the few times she actually told Rokula how she really felt because the birthday incident was definitely the last straw. She broke up with him for good.

It had been three years from the time they met until the time they broke up. "The Count" tried to win her back with promises, flowers and apologies, but this time his attempts failed.

Gwen realized two entire years later – after the shock and emotional devastation eased up – that Rokula was truly a psychopathological narcissist with unusual paranormal manifestations. He had a way of putting on the mask of a savior, but in the next moment he could be a murderer. Gwen admitted to seeing his face shapeshift into a lizard-like form on a few occasions, but at first she didn't trust her perceptions.

I asked Gwen for more details about the odd shapeshifting images. "His face would sort of have these like heat waves coming from it," she said. "It also appeared as if these tendrils

## Chapter 8: Case Files, Category Four

or something would appear when he was right in my face like for a kiss or something. He had fat cheeks and a snake-like appearance, and his pupils would turn to slits. He had a sneaky smile." But when she confided in others who knew him they also admitted to her that they saw in him similar shapeshifting features. Gwen knew that there was something very, very scary about Rokula.

Drawing by Gwen of Rokula's 'Snakey Face.' Used with permission.

In January 2010, Gwen had a bad car accident. This was a near replay of the disturbing dream both of them had over two years prior. Gwen thinks that somehow Rokula caused her car accident via some form of black magic. Rokula continued to email and text her, even two years after they broke up, saying things like, "I'm dying without you. Live so I can live."

Gwen is still recovering from the trauma and emotional devastation from the Dark Side of Cupid relationship with Rokula. She recalls, "It is the shock that hits the hardest. There were too many unexplainable things, his brainwashing, emotional ups and downs, energy drains, paranormal anomalies and downright psychopathic behaviors. It was like he was sent to literally destroy me."

It's hard to believe such people like Rokula exist in this world, but they do. Gwen questioned her own sanity, but finally started to heal when others she knew started observing similar things with him. Gwen said that there would have been no way she could even begin to heal from this relationship had it not been for the opportunity to tell her story.

"It's amazing how many people's lives are in ruins because of these things and how few people know what's going on. If it weren't for God and being able to tell my story, I would have never come this far healing. Not sure I would have made it this far, period.

"People need to know these kinds of psychopaths exist in the world who put on the masquerade that they are healers, preachers or benevolent gurus. But they are exactly the opposite. Beware of the wolves in sheep's clothing. Oops, I mean lizards in human clothing."

Chapter 9

# Variations on the Dark Side of Cupid: Cupid's Interference and Disruption in Love Relationships

Over the years, I have come across cases where a person or couple claims that the love relationship they want or are already involved in becomes thwarted by an unseen intelligent force. Either the person they want to date somehow becomes manipulated, or the plans to get together are consistently disrupted by situations that seem out of their control. This theme is reminiscent of the movie, *The Adjustment Bureau*, where the lovers are constantly interfered with by supernatural angel "Watchers" who seek to prevent their love affair from happening. In the two following cases, the reporting partners believed their relationship to be broken up by alien beings.

In the first case, the respondent believed that the aliens are Greys who constantly interfered with her, preventing her from establishing a satisfying relationship with a man of her choice. It is common in alien abductee testimonies, and in private support group discussions, for abductees to believe their partners to have been chosen for them by their alien handlers.

In the second of these cases, we seem to have a good cop/bad cop drama. The good ETs set up the soul mate love affair, while the bad ETs break them apart in favor of another, non-soul mate, love bite partner. This is what I call the counterfeit soul mate set-up, as opposed to the real deal.

I have often wondered whether true soul mates can be prevented from meeting, as if their union is a threat to the Watchers. In my work with anomalous trauma, many people who have awakened spiritually believe that a form of spiritual

> **I have often wondered whether true soul mates can be prevented from meeting, as if their union is a threat to the Watchers.**

warfare is happening to prevent a consciousness-raising effect in the world. One common factor in each of my Dark Side of Cupid cases is that all the individuals were involved in the alternative research, paranormal, conspiracy and/or spirituality circles. In other words, all these people were part of a larger consciousness-raising movement in the global community.

*Paige and Aaron*

Paige, an inquisitive, sensitive, twenty-something athlete met Aaron, a good-looking college student her age through a mutual friend. They hit it off one weekend while he was in town and Paige felt a strong attraction to him. On their first date, they kissed. After the first kiss however, Paige lost her voice, making communications between them difficult.

"That was like a precursor and foreshadowing," said Paige, "to manipulated communication between us that would take place in the future. I also had weird stomachaches and diarrhea. That week I got really sick and my voice was still raspy, and when he called it was hard because I was tired and could still barely talk. We had a very strong bond but slowly I could feel it unraveling due to outside manipulated circumstances. I was in love and his feelings were fading, making it feel like unrequited love."

Paige had dreams during this time, which indicated to her some message that another presence was trying to meddle. She dreamed of robbers and thieves who kept trying to interfere, chase her, and who poked, prodded, and inserted implants into her. When she became lucid within the dream and identified these beings as hackers and disruptors, their dream behaviors sped up as if to "hurry on what they were doing."

Was this a red flag that her love life was indeed being interfered with?

Paige was aware of the paranormal anomalies and unusual disruptions, but Aaron was not. Cell phones were constantly being accidentally damaged, lost or not working so she couldn't connect with him. Phone messages and text messages disappeared. Internet forum messages were deleted or intercepted even though they were posted. She could never get through to him.

When asked if she felt unusual emotional draining due to the disrupted love relationship she said, "When I was talking to Aaron he suddenly got this glazed look in his eyes, and for the next twenty minutes he talked to me in a way where he was trying to reject the original emotional tone from liking me and a mutual connection to one of rejection. It's like I got this draining feeling as if the flow of the conversation was taken away, and his emotional state shifted as if some implant or unseen force activated him. And for that period of time, during that part of the conversation, he said things that made me feel brushed off and as if he didn't like me. Then the next day, he did not recall that part of the conversation, as if 'something else' took him over to say these things, which elicited feelings of rejection and a shift from emotional connection, friendliness and attraction to one of being shunned. Basically from feeling good to feeling 'bad' suddenly."

I asked Paige about synchronicities, omens, or odd dreams during this time. She confirmed this and added:

"There were tons of synchronicities, paranormal events, entity visitations and odd dreams that occurred during this time. The main point is that I was aware of these things and he was clueless, just going along his life on autopilot. Cell phones were constantly being damaged: dropping in the pool, hot tub, toilet, ocean, Gatorade being spilled on it, my number disappearing out of their phone and vice versa. Not receiving calls, dropped calls, bad connection, battery dying at the most critical times, etc. Electronics were messed with, including car trouble, social network messages on the Internet being manipulated and others. I used to have dreams that he would call me and then he would call me that day, and I would have my hand on the phone about to call him and then my phone would ring and it was him. I have an intuitive sense when the guy's personality is his 'true self' and when he is 'affected.' I use the term affected when he is not acting to true character whether it be from entity possession, implants, mind control or other methods of manipulation."

Paige told me that this kind of thing has happened with others, as if the unseen watchers don't want her to get involved with certain men. She said, "It's something I recognize and can become aware of because of its shift in emotional tone, the glazed look in their eyes and behaviors which are out of character for them, and which leave me feeling bad, hurt or rejected, and disrupted. And they often "forget" what they said or did during this glazed over time period."

Paige developed a growing, emerging awareness and enhanced lucid dreaming ability following what she described as a kundalini awakening experience in 2006. In her "red flag" dreams where robbers were chasing her, Paige started to notice patterns to these dream-hacking assailants.

"The beings who look and act like robbers, became this way in the dreams after I started questioning what they were doing, and who were they? At first, the dream theme would go along more slowly, then I started getting a weird feeling, and when I got lucid, then I suddenly could see that they were 'robbers' and they no longer could sustain the image of just regular humans or whatever – it was like my own mind could symbolically tell me in the dream that they were robbers of some sort. Then after the image shifted, they behaved much more rapidly and the dream became faster paced with respect to what they were after. They started chasing me, and trying to stick things in me like implants or anything that they really wanted to tag me, so it was easier for them to do what they came to do – in the dream. I end up fighting them, and then would wake up from the dream. They were not sexual dreams, but have been happening for about ten years, these 'dream hackers.'"

She now practices meditation and involves herself in consciousness raising studies. Paige is motivated to understand the universe, spirituality, and higher consciousness. She hasn't been able to thwart the love relationship disruptors completely, but has learned a great deal for such a young woman.

*Becky and Cecil*

Becky, a life long alien abductee, contacted me shortly after my first book, *The Love Bite*, was published. She related to me a love relationship she had been in for five years that had been set up and then manipulated and interfered with consistently by beings whom she and her partner believed could be extraterrestrials, both good and bad. Both individuals are exceptionally sensitive and psychic. Becky said that after she did a cleansing detoxification and started ingesting clean energy foods, herbs, and non-fluoridated water, her extrasensory perceptive abilities increased.

Becky was still involved with her ex-husband, Darren, when she met Cecil through a coincidence involving a mysterious credit card that arrived in the mail. Becky had not ordered the card, but it enabled Darren to enroll in some college courses, where he met Cecil. Cecil had received dream messages from two "etheric beings" that told him to partner up with Darren in a class assignment. Cecil did not even like Darren. He asked his etheric dream messengers, "Why?"

They said, "Just go with him for now. We need you to. It is very important. We will explain later."

One evening Darren brought Cecil home with him and

offered him a beer. Becky told me:

"When I saw Cecil that evening, I was extremely attracted to him. When we met each other it was incredible for both of us. It was love at first sight and a feeling of 'where have you been?' Cecil said that I sparked every filament of his being and that I lit up like a small sun. Then Cecil told me later that at that time, his watchers said to him that he was to rescue me because the bad aliens were trying to kill me. I had health problems at the time, so I believe this. They ordered me to go to his house via very strong and loud beeps that I heard in my inner ears."

Becky continued, "The first time we made love it was and is always incredible. We are like a lock and key. I feel that way and so does he. We fit perfectly in every way, physically, emotionally, with all of our senses. We truly think it is possible we are soul mates."

Cecil believed that Becky and he were meant to be together. What is odd is that before Cecil met Becky he had a girlfriend whom he described as the antithesis of Becky. He had spent ten horrible years with this other woman, who resembled Becky but seemed to him like a false soul mate. In fact, he believed his relationship with her had been designed and arranged by the bad ETs in order to sabotage his meeting with Becky – his true soul mate – when that did occur. She was like a cardboard cutout of Becky and, according to Cecil, was heavily puppetized by the bad ETs.

Becky told me that one of the ways that the bad ET watchers interfere with them is through their dreams. The themes will be such that they wake up in a bad mood, feel angry, or experience any manner of negative emotions. She said:

"They come up with new stuff as soon as there is a chink in our armor, in our relationship, so to speak. As soon as we question or doubt something ourselves, they will try and manipulate that. It's like they battle with you in your dreams

*Chapter 9: Variations of the Dark Side of Cupid*

> **Who is in charge here? Are the watchers the same ancient mythical gods who needed to be supplicated and appeased in nearly all ancient religions? Or could extraterrestrials be interloping as these gods?**

all night long, leaving you exhausted. But Cecil and I have learned to communicate now and share what they are trying to impose, so they don't succeed."

Becky said that these beings, which have appeared to them like dark energy blobs, radiate extremely negative energy. "We know their motivation is to create chaos in our relationship." These malevolent beings have sabotaged every business endeavor they've attempted by manipulating the people Becky and Cecil interacted with.

Becky added:

"This has been going on for four-and-a-half years and it's been exhausting. We've been unable to keep a job steadily, so we've been financially destitute. It's been nuts, to say the least. But with our faith in Jesus, many of these interferences have stopped. No amount of spiritual fighting ourselves has stopped it. Instead it's only left us exhausted because they just bring in stronger guns, so to speak. Learn what your thoughts are, and what are not. And communicate with each other. Always. Build unit integrity."

It hasn't been easy to stay together. Becky said that she and Cecil had broken up three times in five years. But each time they got back together and their love has only gotten stronger. Asked who these watchers are and why they are doing this, Becky answered, "either the watchers have manipulated our past lives and present to torture, experiment and observe like science lab rats – how humans behave in the matters of the heart – or we are truly soul mates. The good

ETs assisted in our meeting, and the bad ones do not want the love frequency on the planet so we become their targets in earnest."

Perhaps there is a war going on between forces of light and dark. The dark watchers seek to prevent true love and soul mates from connecting. They set up false soul mates to take their place, leaving an emotional wreckage of misery in their path. Perhaps these watchers are playing both sides of the fence like good cop, bad cop. But why? To test our resolve to see how far we will go to follow our heart's true desire?

Does the Dark Cupid want to keep us stupid? Is that the reason for the endless dramas and relationships that don't seem to pan out, or for preventing the quality of love and true soul mate match we desire? Could there really be such a diabolical force working against humanity? Or is this simply our own karma, payback for sins committed in former lifetimes?

In the Kabbalah, there is a belief that there are good forces trying to bring soul mates together, but also negative forces trying to break them apart. An interested correspondent sent me an excerpt by Rabbi Eliyahu da Vidas:

"When a man comes into this world without a heavy debt to rectify, he may meet his soul mate and marry her without much effort. The Ari cites the case of a man who sins and has to reincarnate, whereas his soul mate has completed her task in this world and has no further need of reincarnation.[*] In special cases his soul mate is allowed to incarnate with him, and she will come back to this world with him in order to help him. When the time comes for him to get married, however, he will not find her effortlessly as in the first case, but after an intense search and struggle. Since he reincarnated because of a sin he committed, the accusers on high speak against him; they want him to be prevented from meeting her, on the

---

[*] Sha"ar Ha Gilgulim, 20

ground that he does not deserve it. So they spread animosity between the couple and they later quarrel. That is why it is written that making couples is as difficult as splitting the Red Sea!"

I find it interesting the Watchers in this reference are referred to as "accusers on high." Why accuse humans of being undeserving of love? Who is in charge here? Are the watchers the same ancient mythical gods who needed to be supplicated and appeased in nearly all ancient religions? Or could extraterrestrials be interloping as these gods?

# Chapter 10

# Alien Abduction Cases with Diabolical Variations of the Love Bite Theme

The late abduction researcher, Barbara Bartholic, in addition to having examined classic alien-hybrid scenarios and medical exams (so popularized in alien abduction literature), also investigated many alien abduction reports involving themes of love obsession and energy vampirism. She shared three of her cases with me in 1999, while I was writing my first book, *The Love Bite*.

Yet, I omitted them from that book. In part, they were just too taboo. Certainly they were not making the rounds in the lecture circuit. These kinds of reports were usually swept under the rug by researchers. In the first place, they do not fit into the alien-grey hybrid medical scenarios recapitulated in alien abduction research. Nor do they accord with the popular notion of neutral or benevolent ETs, especially the consciousness-raising variety promoted by New Age ideology.

I am including these cases here, however. One reason is that they show a clear overlap, and probable connection, between classic alien abduction themes and occult paranormal vampirism themes. Also, they represent the range and degree to which some alien abductions involve relationship set-ups, break-ups, sexuality changes, or love obsessions. In all of these cases, a relationship was either broken up, or set up with love obsession themes. In particular, they included supernatural elements that revealed the psychic vampiric nature of the predatory aliens. The aliens in these cases demonstrate an obvious malevolent nature.

It is my opinion that the abducting alien beings are

engaged in a campaign of deception against the human race in the form of psychic vampirism. They seek to feed off the human soul, to oppress it and, in some cases, to engage in demonic possession.

*The Case of Andrea and Brian*

This abduction report occurred during a wave of UFO activity in the Midwest USA in December of 1988. This case demonstrates how a married woman's alien abduction was followed by an infatuation with another man, disrupting her marriage and family. This progressed into a complete personality shift and intermittent demonic possession.

In late 1987, several states in the Midwest experienced a wave of UFO activity that included areas in Arkansas, Texas, Alabama, Florida, Missouri, Kansas and Oklahoma. In a rural area outside of a major city in Oklahoma, Barbara investigated reports from thirty people who were involved in UFO sightings and abduction experiences during this "alien invasion," as she called it.

Andrea, a beautiful 24-year-old married woman and mother of two children, experienced an alien abduction around midnight in December 1988, during this wave of UFO activity.

She awoke to the sounds of her son Robby crying, but went back to sleep. Next, she awoke to the sight of a white cloud over her face, which somehow compelled her to get up and walk out through the front door. Andrea described walking through the front door as though it were liquid glass. She then continued onward, walking out to the gate towards their three-acre pasture. There, she saw a small creature with glowing green eyes, but felt no fear. The entity told her that his name was Nasha, and that he was an apparition.

Then the cloud disappeared from her face, and all Andrea could remember was feeling temporarily paralyzed, her feet sinking into the ground. Eventually she got back inside, but woke up the next morning feeling extremely exhausted and with a flu-like respiratory condition. Her husband, Brian, did not believe the story of her alien encounters, explaining it away as her imagination.

Within a few days of the incident, Andrea's home seemed to be the epicenter of a very strange quake. Neighbors also felt it, which was described as a loud underground explosion of some kind. The night before, some nearby residents had seen a UFO.

Andrea then called Barbara to report her experience. When Barbara came to meet her, they discussed the recent events, but what really struck Barbara was something else. This was

> **It is my opinion that the abducting alien beings are engaged in a campaign of deception against the human race in the form of psychic vampirism. They seek to feed off the human soul, to oppress it and, in some cases, to engage in demonic possession.**

Andrea's sudden infatuation with a homosexual male with whom she had previously been friends, but nothing more.

Then, some time later, Andrea discovered that she was pregnant. At the time of her abduction, her husband had been out of town for several weeks. During the entire month, they had sexual relations just once. Andrea did not want another baby; she was already caring for her three-month old son, and did not feel she was in a condition to have another child. She visited a doctor, who performed an abortion.

The doctor estimated the fetus to be nine and a half weeks, which fit into the timing of Andreas's encounter with the entity Nasha. Furthermore, Andrea believed this baby could have been the offspring of the man she had become infatuated with, something she believed would have been arranged during her abduction.

Andrea's ongoing infatuation with her homosexual friend caused more and more friction in her marriage with Brian. Eventually, it led to a separation.

A few months later, Andrea called Barbara again to report a frightening alien visitation with the Nasha creature. At first, Andrea thought it was a dream. She had heard her son cry and rushed to his bedroom. To her horror, she saw Nasha lifting her son out of his bed. Andrea described this alien as barely four feet tall. Mostly, she recalled his eyes, which were large, glowing, green, and wrapped around the side of his head. They reminded her of the eyes of a large fly or insect.

All she could remember was yelling, "No, he's mine!" Nasha claimed that Robby belonged to them – the aliens. Some sort of argument or fight ensued between Andrea and Nasha. The next morning Andrea had intense itching in her vaginal area. It was so severe that she had to apply hot compresses, and in doing so, she noticed two puncture holes on her labial fold. They were complete holes, side by side, about a half-inch apart, as if she had been punctured with a paper puncher.

Extremely upset by the painful injury, Andrea visited five different doctors to find the cause of such an anomaly. Brian continued to disbelieve Andrea. He assumed the holes were simply some kind of after effect of having recently given birth. He thought she was losing her mind.

Within one month of Andrea's visit to the clinic regarding this problem, the medical records describing it completely disappeared. From that time onward, her life started falling apart, and she displayed a drastic personality change.

Andrea had previously been a caring person, happily married, and a good mother. Now, according to her longtime friend Samantha, everything changed. She began drinking, became abusive and angry, and became a liar and thief. Even her facial appearance changed to a blank stare without muscle tone. Eventually, she abandoned everything and everyone she knew.

At the time she told all this to Barbara, Samantha – one of Andrea's close friends – had not known of Andrea's UFO and alien encounters. She simply said, "I looked at her and I couldn't look into her eyes, because the person I was looking at was not the same Andrea I knew. That was not Andrea in Andrea's body."

This went on for more than three years. One of Andrea's more noticeable changes was in her sexual behavior. First she had been a monogamous housewife, then obsessed with a homosexual man, then abstained from sex altogether, and then had numerous sexual partners.

"Sometimes," Samantha said, "Andrea appeared to come out of this personality-shifted state, but then she'd return to heavy drinking and lose touch again."

Then, three years after her initial call to Barbara in 1988, Andrea phoned again, this time just minutes after another alien contact in her apartment.

She had just returned from a dinner date at 7:30 p.m., undressed and lay down for a nap. She sensed a presence in the room, but took a nap anyway. The next thing she recalled was awakening very irritated. She got up to use the bathroom and was shocked to find that her stomach was bloated and distended. On her legs was a series of straight scratches, three-inches long each, from her knees down to her ankles. There were about twelve of them, all perfectly identical.

Petrified and in shock, Andrea called Barbara. "They were just here," she said. She didn't know what to do. Barbara packed up her video camera and recording equipment and rushed over to Andrea's apartment, accompanied by her husband, Bob. They were there within 25 minutes.

Meanwhile, Andrea took a shower. Most oddly, by the time of Barbara's arrival, she had forgotten what she said on the phone.

Barbara and Bob saw the bruising, scratches, and body marks. On Andreas's stomach was carved a design that included the symbol of a fish. On her thighs were two distinct triangles and long scratch lines covering the full length of the thigh. Peculiar bumps appeared on her wrist aligned in a pattern. On Andreas's thigh was etched a large one inch equilateral triangle, and three inches above that was another symbol of a fish. During Barbara's investigation she had trouble with her camera and recording equipment, as if there were an interfering energy field present. Odd sounds could be heard in the apartment and were recorded on the original videotape; the sounds of a deep, pulsating, rhythmic hum.

They found what looked like claw marks going from Andrea's breast to under her arm, and many scratch lines on her breast as well. The symbol of a fish on Andrea's stomach had inscripted within it the letter h. Barbara recognized this symbol as one being present in the experience of another contactee, Riley Martin, while aboard a mother ship.

After Barbara videotaped Andrea's body marks, she left the bedroom to allow Andrea to get dressed again. It took longer than expected. Realizing how traumatizing the evening had been, Barbara decided to look in on Andrea. Walking into the bedroom, she heard fumbling, raspy sounds coming from the closet. There Andrea was, crouched down on all fours, growling like an animal. This was not Andrea in Andrea's body. This seemed to be a classic demonic possession, taking place right before Barbara's eyes.

Barbara left the room and took out a piece of paper from her purse. This contained some passages from the Bible; it just so happened she had recently attended a service and had written them down. Barbara brought Bob into the room – she knew he would not easily believe her otherwise. Then, walking toward the closet, she reciting the scriptures with authority, rebuking the invading entity in the name of Jesus. However, her words seemed to have no effect. Whatever was inside Andrea remained oblivious to Barbara's words and showed no fear. The video camera also stopped running for no apparent reason.

Meanwhile, for the next twenty minutes, Andrea continued to thrash about on all fours like an animal. Finally, she ran out of the closet, screaming, "It's all over me! It's all over me!"

After much effort, Barbara calmed her down. She asked Andrea if she remembered anything. Andrea did not, but said she felt a presence. When probed further, she did not want to discuss it.

Barbara tried to soothe Andrea and educate her on the reality of alien abductions. She mentioned the other local abductee – the homosexual man she had become infatuated with – who had witnessed Andrea on the ship with Nasha. (This is what is often described as joint abductions remembered by independent witnesses. Oftentimes they are merely remembered as mutually shared dreams). Barbara offered some suggestions to Andrea about incorporating some kind of shield or spiritual protection against such assaults, as it is helpful for some people. Barbara mentioned that the use of Jesus Christ's name sometimes is effective in dispersing these negative entities. But her advice fell on deaf ears. Andrea did not feel comfortable using Jesus's name.

That night, Andrea remained alone in her apartment, despite Barbara's offer to stay with her. She had to work the next morning. Everything was fine, she said.

A few nights after this bizarre and frightening event, Andrea's estranged husband, Brian, arranged to meet with her after work one evening at a local bar. He was worried about Andrea, and invited Samantha to go along. They arrived at around 11:30 p.m., but an hour later, Andrea was arguing with Brian outside the bar. Her anger soon escalated, and Brian and Samantha could only watch as Andrea went into one of her tirades, yelling and striking at Brian. Then she completely lost control, falling to the ground and rolling around the grass like a dog, right in front of the bar entrance.

Through the 1990s, Samantha made several more attempts

to meet with Andrea, but Andrea generally avoided contact. She continued to go from heavy drinking to sobering up, only to return to drinking. Aware of a problem, she wanted to work things out with her husband, but just could not confront or resolve the issues in their relationship. Although Andrea could still function enough to hold down a job, she continued to have alien abductions. As of 1999, when Barbara last had contact from her, her marriage with Brian remained unreconciled.

*The Psychologist and the Shadow People*

This case came to the attention of Barbara Bartholic in 1998 by a contactee named LeeAnn, who lived in a Midwestern U.S. state. LeeAnn had been friends with a psychologist named Barry Smith (pseud.) and his wife for one year, and they communicated regularly by email and telephone. LeeAnn had met Barry through his son, who was also a contactee. In fact, it was LeeAnn's and Barry's mutual interests in ET and paranormal experiences that led them to communicate in the first place.

This report unravels the dark influence of interdimensional shadow people. These beings appear to have been in communication with Barry and other people via channeling and automatic writing. They encouraged activities that influenced Barry and his wife to have an open marriage with another couple, all in the effort to produce a "special child." No child was ever conceived. Ultimately, however, these communications resulted in increasing instability, paranoia, and "hauntings" to such an extent that Barry committed suicide.

For the past two years, Barry told LeeAnn, he had felt different about himself. He suddenly became interested in things that had previously held no interest for him, things such as the paranormal. He began receiving thoughts and telepathic messages. He even wondered if a "walk-in" spirit had entered him. Still, none of this seemed to bother him at the time.

While Barry corresponded with LeeAnn, he and his wife were living with a couple, whom we will call Mr. and Mrs. X, and their three children. (Barry's son was grown and living on his own by this time.) They lived in Florida within view of the NASA facility where Mr. X worked. Barry and his wife had become good friends with the X family as a result of Barry's work as a clinical psychologist with learning disabled children. This included the autistic son of Mr. and Mrs. X.

According to LeeAnn, Mr. X had become aware of having what he believed were extraterrestrial encounters during the previous four years. As the two couples developed their friendship, they engaged in channeling and automatic writing, and collectively received telepathic messages from beings claiming to be aliens. Apparently, these beings communicated the idea that it was important for them to produce another child. The problem was that Barry's wife could no longer have children, nor could Mr. X father a child. As a consequence, it was decided that Barry and Mrs. X would have sexual relations until she conceived this special child.

The couples decided to move in together into one household so that they could have this child and live together as one family. The three children were apparently not aware that their parents were having sex with other partners for this special child project. According to LeeAnn, this arrangement was not the result of any kind of extramarital affair, but in full agreement between the participating couples.

The extraterrestrial communications further urged the families to move to the mountains, where this special child would be safe in the future. They even made plans to move to Colorado. But this is when things really began to unravel.

Starting around January 1998, according to LeeAnn, Barry began experiencing kidney pain, and increasingly used alcohol to relieve it. LeeAnn knew that Barry was drinking, although he never wrote any communications that appeared as though he were intoxicated.

Chapter 10: Alien Abduction Cases

For some time, Barry and LeeAnn had shared some anomalous experiences. Now, about a month before he took his life, they had a mutually shared dream. LeeAnn described her version of it:

> "I am driving my ambulance (I am an EMT) on a foggy night. I can see an orange streetlight on the corner across the street from a hill where a house stood. I could see a man walking towards me. I see that it is Barry and say, 'Barry, what are you doing here?'
>
> "He hops into the ambulance and they drive to a nearby hospital. The hospital is full of dark hallways except for bare light bulbs on the ceiling above every 20 or 30 feet. The lighting was odd in that it didn't reflect very far, like it was being absorbed. You could only see close to the light source. I could see that the walls were white tiles, and a hard cement floor. We walked by some partitioned off stalls that had beds in them. They looked similar to emergency room stalls and beds with a curtain partitioning each stall, except no other equipment besides beds.
>
> "We decide to stretch out and rest for a while. Then a woman with dark, shoulder length hair wearing all white comes out of nowhere screaming at us, accusing us of having sex! We told her we did not and that was the end of the dream."

Barry recalled the same dream (it is common for abductees to have shared dreams), and added that the house on the hill near the orange streetlight was actually his house in Florida. LeeAnn's description of the street and house was a perfect match, although she was not aware of this at the time. Barry also recalled the hospital scene with the screaming dark haired woman, the stalls and beds, although not the ambulance ride to the hospital.

Not long after LeeAnn and Barry's mutually shared dream,

Barry started to sense shadow-like beings in his home and bedroom. So did other family members, especially the children who also had bedrooms upstairs. To Barry, they appeared as shadowy outlines in human form that would fade into nothing. He could sense their presence, as if they were always there, watching.

Problems with neighbors across the street also began to develop at this time. These neighbors started arguing with the family about minor issues until a great deal of tension and chaos had grown.

Barry also noticed a car constantly parked in front of the house across the street, which never moved. He looked into it one day and saw suspicious-looking radio equipment. He thought these might be surveillance gadgets and wondered if he were being spied upon. Although he let the matter go, he told LeeAnn that he was keeping all of his unusual experiences, telepathic messages, and observations in a journal. Because of the nearness of the NASA facility and the suspicions of surveillance, LeeAnn and Barry both wondered whether a diabolical mind control experiment was being conducted on the couples.

As his kidney pain worsened, Barry drank more. Two weeks before his last communication, he decided to go "cold turkey" from the alcohol to see if his pain would ease as a result. It did not, however.

All this was made worse by Barry's growing awareness of the shadow people. About a week before he took his life, his communications grew more alarming. According to LeeAnn, he was seeing them every day. It got to the point where the children in Barry's household were afraid to go to bed, as they could also see the shadow people at night.

Barry told LeeAnn that the shadow people were threatening him, even becoming violent. He said they implanted visions in his mind of Greys having sex with his wife as they laughed and mocked him, inciting rage and jealousy. They made it clear

> **On the last night of Barry's life, he emailed LeeAnn. "Are these beings real?," he asked. "Am I going crazy? They are trying to kill my family, aren't they?"**

that they could do anything they wanted, and he was helpless to stop them. He was terrified of them. Yet Barry continued to write about them, including his thoughts on who they were and how they might have been the aliens he, his wife, and Mr. and Mrs. X had been communicating with all along.

On the last night of Barry's life, he emailed LeeAnn. "Are these beings real?," he asked. "Am I going crazy? They are trying to kill my family, aren't they?"

LeeAnn sensed something was terribly wrong. Near midnight, she tried to contact him, but only reached Mrs. X. Barry had just gone to bed.

Three hours later, at 3:00 a.m., Barry woke up, reached for his gun, put it to his head, and shot himself.

Later, Mrs. X told LeeAnn that on the night of Barry's death she had heard him yelling upstairs, all alone in the bedroom. She went up to see what he was yelling at, and saw Barry shouting, apparently at the shadow beings. "No," he screamed, "I'm not going to do that!" But she saw no other beings in the room.

Mrs. X had never gotten pregnant, and the family never moved to the mountains as they were urged to do. LeeAnn kept in contact with Mrs. X, inquiring about Barry's journal writings. Mrs. X found nothing other than a computer disk with some of his writings, but apparently missing various entries. According to LeeAnn, "Whatever was in those writings was an account of what and who he believed the aliens to really be."

Barry's autopsy report showed no kidney problems. Nor

was there evidence of hallucinations or DTs (delirium tremens) from alcohol withdrawal or liver damage, as one might have expected from the heavy drinking.

This story sheds light on possible deception concerning the nature of some of these alleged extraterrestrials. Barry's enthusiasm about the extraterrestrials turned to fear when he began experiencing threats from "shadow people," whom he later believed to be the entities behind the telepathic messages and promptings to have this "special child." Shortly after Barry claimed to have discovered the true nature of these beings, he killed himself in obvious distress. There are elements of a possible human surveillance team and timely chaos during the period of Barry's discoveries about these shadow people, which seems to point to efforts to prevent him from revealing what he knew.

At the time of LeeAnn's interview with Barbara Bartholic, she had not been feeling well, and complained of extreme sleepiness and bizarre dreams following Barry's death, including recurring themes of being chased by MIBs (Men In Black). Fortunately, these soon ended. By 1999, LeeAnn had put the incident behind her.

## Mariah and the Seductive Spirit Guide

Mariah, a married mother of three, came to Barbara Bartholic in late 1985, following a harrowing love obsession two years after a UFO abduction experience. Mariah was referred to Barbara from a local psychologist who knew about Barbara's work with alien abductees.

Mariah's case involves classic alien abduction medical exams, a miraculous healing, automatic writing, telepathic messages from otherworldly beings, and contact with a spirit guide claiming to be the deceased country singer, Jim Reeves. A love obsession ensued between Mariah and the spirit guide. This, combined with the constant contact with channeled entities, drove Mariah over the edge until she broke down and received psychiatric help. Had it not been for Barbara, Mariah might not have survived this ordeal. She expressed deep gratitude for Barbara's compassion and support.

This case is not for the faint hearted. The emotional/psychic vampirism and psychological instability caused by all this escalated to such a level that we are really talking about demonic possession.

That alone is an important reason why this case stayed in the dungeons of secrecy until now. Most of the UFO community, and especially the New Age crowds, would not allow it. In fact, during the early 1990s, when Barbara tried to discuss this case at a UFO conference, she was scoffed off stage by a well-known disclosure speaker. He refused to believe that "malevolent reptilian ETs exist." For many, their attachment to benevolent space brother ET contact belief systems are too firmly affixed to their egos.

Mariah, her husband, and Barbara are all deceased, and this is the only reason I can now tell this story, using pseudonyms to protect the surviving family members.

This story needs to be told as it unfolded.

When I received this case in 1999, Mariah was 59 years old, married, and a mother of eight children. She was of Cherokee and Irish descent, very intelligent, and multi-talented. Her first anomalous event occurred at the age of five, following a fall in which she broke her leg and jaw. During the fall, she became aware of being embraced by a warm white light.

Years later, a doctor who examined her asked, "How could you have walked around in so much pain?" The physician showed her an X-ray of her neck. It showed how some of her vertebrae were fused together where her neck had been broken. For some reason, Mariah had been able to function with a broken neck without much notice.

At age ten, Mariah's tonsils were removed. Before the procedure, as she was receiving ether, she saw herself lifted from her body by a beautiful golden light. She saw beings who took her by the hands, called her by her full name and said, "We have been waiting for you."

Oddly, the facial profiles of these beings were in the shape of a question mark. They wore what looked like black skullcaps over their heads, giving the effect of a widow's peak hairline. Later in this story, as we shall see, Mariah encountered these same beings in connection to what appeared to be classic ET contact, as well as in a spirit guide capacity, except that in this case they were impersonators. This observation is noteworthy because some individuals who participated in DMT-induced mystical experiences also encountered alien like beings, experienced apparent alien abductions, and had out-of-body experiences.*

Mariah's husband, Clyde, was a medical corpsman in the Air Force. As a result, throughout their marriage and her adult life, they moved frequently. In 1965, Clyde was stationed at Kelly Air Force Base in Texas. There, they saw several UFOs and anomalous lights, on one occasion even witnessing a dogfight of UFOs over the base. At another time, while stationed in Greece, a greenish-yellow light followed Mariah and Clyde as they drove in their car. Neither recalled any abductions or missing time.

It wasn't until Mariah was married with several young children that she experienced a full blown UFO abduction, replete with missing time and unexplained physical after-effects.

On September 23, 1972, at 10:30 p.m., Mariah drove to her night job as a nurse's aid at a parochial school convent in an affluent area of Tulsa, Oklahoma. She drove to the end of a road in a wooded area that was roughly one-quarter mile from her home. The first four blocks of the main street seemed to be

---

* See, for instance, Rick Straussman, M.D., *DMT: The Spirit Molecule* (Park Street Press, 2001).

unusually deserted.

Then matters became a bit strange. The next thing Mariah remembered was being on a two-lane road in an undeveloped area four miles away. She had no memory of how she got there.

She arrived at work an hour and a half late, even though the drive should have taken only ten minutes. Mariah had no memory of what had happened, although she vaguely remembered driving in her car, looking at her hands, and wondering, "What did they do to my hands?" The reaction of the convent sisters was also unusual. Normally very strict, on this occasion they said nothing about Mariah's tardiness.

Concerned about her missing time, Mariah feared she might have had a petit mal epileptic seizure, even though she was not epileptic. She went to the emergency room the following day, and the attending doctor ordered some electroencephalograph tests. The first EEG came out abnormal, but then when the test was repeated, it came out normal. When the doctor examined Mariah's eyes with a light, she recoiled in excruciating pain, complaining that the light hurt her retinas. The doctor told her, "There's no way your eyes could be hurting."

> **Mariah had no memory of what had happened, although she vaguely remembered driving in her car, looking at her hands, and wondering, "What did they do to my hands?"**

At this point in Mariah's life, she had no knowledge of UFOs much less of alien abductions. In the ensuing weeks, she often woke up at night with flashbacks of the abduction. Staring at her hands, she continually asked herself, "What have they done to my hands?"

In these flashbacks, Mariah saw herself returning to her car in a rural area. Her car was pulled over. She walked towards her vehicle and could see humanoid figures, guards of some sort, watching her as she returned to her car. They acted as if in approval of her. Mariah also saw a female figure with dark shoulder length hair in a silver jumpsuit, as well as two males with dark hair. One male was normal height for a man, with curly, shorthaired blonde hair, wearing a white jumpsuit with a Neru, mandarin type of collar. He appeared to be an officer of some type. Mariah received the message in her mind, "All is well. You are free to go." Her next memory in the flashback was of driving to her job. At an intersection, she briefly recalled the abduction, but it was all so confusing. She could only think about how she had left her son's shoes at her mother's house, and this was why she was so late to work. Yet Mariah knew that she had not left his shoes there, and that she was being confused by nonsensical thoughts in her mind. She was extremely tired.

But beyond the flashbacks was the miracle of her hands. For a long time, Mariah had suffered from a terrible case of rheumatoid arthritis. Now, however, her hands were completely healed. Just as dramatic was her sudden increase in psychic abilities.

All of these sudden developments prompted her to consult a psychiatrist. The professional she consulted had no knowledge of alien visitations or UFO abduction phenomena. He performed a hypnotic regression to find the probable cause of Mariah's distress. Under hypnosis, this is what she recalled:

> "I found myself in a tall plexiglass-like cylinder that was like a large test tube. I was naked, unable to move, but could see a cobalt blue light emanating from the bottom of the tube. The light came up around me almost like a sterilization or cleansing effect. The thought occurred to me, "I wonder if this is what it's like to be a test tube baby.
>
> "I wasn't afraid. I wondered where in the hell I was. Then the next thing I remember, I was lying on

*Chapter 10: Alien Abduction Cases*

an examining table with a tall blonde man on my left side. He was wearing a small Neru-type collar. I didn't understand their speech, but they spoke telepathically and told me I could be communicating by way of symbols. And then I could translate that according to my understanding of language. The tall blond man (human looking) told me I had nothing to fear. I felt no fear whatsoever. As a matter of fact, I don't think I felt love, but I fell in lust with the blond being.

"I was then taken to another area where I was monitored by some kind of X-ray machine, like a CAT scan that pictured all of my organs. Then they took me to another room that looked like a pre-natal nursery. They explained to me that virgin births take place throughout the universe and especially in our own galaxy. The babies start out as female and if they want a male they take a semen specimen from a male and inject it into the fetus at a particular time of gestation. In a matter of four-five months it develops into a full-blown baby that looks like a nine-month old full term baby. I felt very comfortable and secure about this event. I was not threatened in any way.

"The aliens all wore goggles or lenses over their eyes and some type of caps over their heads. Some of the aliens wore light fitting bathing caps that were black in color and had the shape of a widow's peak hairline. They wore pearly grey, smooth jumpsuits made of a shiny, stretchy spandex type of material. One of the beings was tall with white cottony hair and a bulbous forehead. The others were pleasant looking and they all had four fingers, instead of five. Some of the beings had hair on their heads and were very human looking. They were kind. I had no fear at all. The X–ray machine was shaped like a human body. Some of the lights emitted caused distress but others were soothing. I did not experience any major discomfort even when they were operating on my brain. I did not fear these beings. They were condescending in a courteous manner. They were so advanced that we are as primitives in comparison. My association with them has enhanced both my psychic abilities and my IQ."

In 1972 there had been no public knowledge of alien abductions other than the Betty and Barney Hill case, and Mariah knew nothing of that. It is notable that Mariah described and drew diagrams of a prenatal nursery years before these kinds of reports circulated in UFO abduction research literature.

A year and a half after Mariah's abduction in 1972, she began receiving messages through automatic writing. At the time, she made no connection between these spirit guide messages and the alien beings who abducted her. The messages were from beings who claimed they came from another galaxy, and from Orion's Belt. They claimed to be here looking for emissaries and intermediaries between their race and earth species. They were using different people, they said, and Mariah was one of the chosen few. They did not say why. Nor did they mention her UFO encounter of 1972. As Mariah put it:

> "The messages started with many flatteries. They said I was so intelligent that no one recognized me because I was a higher evolved being. They were evolved enough to recognize a genius, but others of earth couldn't, they weren't advanced enough to recognize one. They helped me feel good about myself. I was one of the few selected as a go between for them and humanity. They made requests, physical ones, and told me my health would get better, but it didn't. My physical health deteriorated and it pulled my mental health down. I didn't eat or sleep or take good care of myself during the periods of automatic writing. It got to the point that I would be led to the typewriter – as it was faster than handwriting. I would spend hours

writing. The entities would give me names and terms to look up which could later be confirmed as exact to detail, sometimes verbatim from the encyclopedias. The guides deliberately gave me high-level information to look up, so that I could trust the information I was getting.

"Some of the writings that came through were of a religious nature. Mother Mary, saints, Jesus and Joan of Arc came through, offering important spiritual information. Sometimes technical information and formulas came, through like the quatrains of Nostradamus and complex formulas to cure cancer."

Mariah was told she was to have a special mission on Earth. She was to be an emissary, picked out from other groups.

The entities told her, "You are not the only one – that would inflate your ego. But you are one of a very few chosen ones. You must let the world know that there are guardians on the planet and they will be coming soon. They will be guarding us, showing us the right things to do. Protect the planet's environment from overkill, so to speak."

According to the messages, one of the main reasons Mariah was selected as a spokesperson was to prepare for the rapture that would soon take place. She was told she was to help gather people to be taken off the planet during the rapture. In Mariah's words, "We would be watching the planet as it was being cleansed. Then to return to the planet and get it prepared for human habitation again."

At one point Mariah asked the entities, "What about my family?" They replied, "Well, your family will be left behind." Mariah objected that she would not. She said she would rather remain on Earth with her family than go with the extraterrestrials.

In addition to the writings, Mariah was shown vivid visions of catastrophes, volcanoes, and earthquakes. She described it as the internal combustion of the Earth. The Earth was like a hard-boiled egg that had been cooked too long and it would just rupture. Mariah was shown these visions from the vantage point of being high up inside a ship overlooking the Earth below.

Not only did Mariah receive messages in writings, but she also could hear the voices telepathically. One particular spirit guide dominated the writings. This spirit claimed to be the deceased country guitar singer, Jim Reeves. Mariah had been repelled by Jim Reeves and his songs, and she had never previously had any interest in him or his music.

In fact, she initially could not remember who he was until the channeled being guided her back to a time in her life when her husband, Clyde, was stationed at a military base far from home. At the time, Clyde was having an affair with a younger woman while Mariah struggled alone to take care of her eight children. Mariah vaguely recalled a particular song of Reeve's that was popular around the same time that Clyde was having the affair. It brought back awful memories of heartbreak which perfectly depicted her situation. She had buried the memory of this song, but was now reminded of it by this being, apparently the deceased spirit of Jim Reeves.

This spirit guide spoke about many topics with Mariah, and often used terms of endearment with her, such as "Lady Bug." He told her that she was to be a spokesperson to the world. He flattered her and made her feel loved. Mariah bought all of Jim Reeves' old records and, despite being unable to read music, learned to play guitar.

"One day," said Mariah, "I was in the front bedroom and my guitar was sitting between the bed and nightstand. By this time, I was able to hear Reeves speak to me telepathically. He said to me. 'Ok lady, let's play.' At that moment, one of Reeves songs started playing on the radio. He kept asking me to play the guitar. Then the strangest thing happened. The guitar was pushed onto the floor by itself."

## Chapter 10: Alien Abduction Cases

There were times when Mariah felt Reeves' hands over her own, guiding her as she played. Sometimes it felt as if his hands were inside of hers.

But this sense of touch did not end there.

The touching progressed into caressing, gentle and loving. To Mariah, it felt completely physical, yet invisible. These caresses developed into kissing and sexual foreplay, an interaction which carried on for several months. Eventually, this deepened into full sexual advances.

"The fondling eventually led to being invited to bed by this spirit," Mariah confessed. "I would physically feel touching, kissing, and even penetration of this spirit into me in full-on sexual intercourse. I could feel everything that was happening, as if he were physically there touching me. I never touched myself and could even see and feel a light pressure on my body and bed as Reeves made love to me."

Mariah carried on a sexual relationship with the Reeves spirit lover for over a year. This was possible in part because of the poor marriage she had with her husband Clyde, who also worked nights. The sexual interaction was so pleasurable that Mariah experienced strong orgasms. Things got to the point where Reeves' spirit presence was constantly with her, as if he were inside of her body and mind.

"By this time," she said, "it was like I became another person. During sexual intercourse I could leave my body and watch. I saw myself as a woman of a slightly darker complexion with long dark hair." But it wasn't simply a matter of seeing this other woman. Sometimes when the Reeves entity was making love to her, Mariah's body was overshadowed by the presence of this woman.

Mariah also began to hear the voices of other spirits, not only Reeves. One of these was of the dark haired woman, and there were others. These voices increased until they became dialogues that were communicating with her.

"When Reeves was not around," Mariah said, "the other

entities gave me messages and suggestions with a sense of urgency. They said I needed to get things done. They wanted me to get information out to the public that the aliens are here to help prepare the Earth for a cleansing, but with a lot of destruction. To teach and tutor the human race how to take care of the planet. I was supposed to travel from here to there, different places to tell and speak about this."

Meanwhile, the sexual advances with the Reeves spirit went on almost daily. Mariah elaborated:

"Sometimes, I was led to bed during the daytime and invited to lie down, to rest and experience true love. I was in an altered state of consciousness. I could see images of other beings during the lovemaking process. Often I was overshadowed by a dark-haired woman while being made love to by Reeves. It was as if the female spirit inside of me was experiencing the sexual passion though me."

On one occasion Mariah was shown a mental image of an enormous ovum being fertilized during sexual intercourse. Later, Mariah was shown a vision of a beautiful baby boy that supposedly was the offspring of Mariah and Reeves in an astral or interdimensional form. Eventually, Mariah was hearing the spirit voices constantly. They began to command her to do things. On one occasion, she was told to cut her hair short like Joan of Arc, one of her favorite saints.

This constant communication and frequent automatic writing, began to drain Mariah. Despite this, she paradoxically experienced a type of hyperactivity. That was when she realized she was getting sick.

"I couldn't handle it," she said. "Sometimes I would get out of the house during the day just to keep away the sexual advances of the Reeves spirit and the constant urges to do automatic writing. One night, after I brought the kids back from their catechism class, I kept hearing voices and got wrapped up in them. It was constant. Then the telepathic voices urged me to do things. As I walked into the kitchen with my children, the voices pressed me to go and grab the boiling pot of coffee on the stove and dowse the scalding coffee over my kids. As I realized the horror of these sudden urges, I pulled back. By this time I knew I was sick."

Thankfully, Mariah did not follow the insane commands to harm her children. She added that while this was happening she could see in her mind's eye a man and woman talking about her. The female voice was the one she saw during the sexual intercourse with Reeves, superimposed over her body. The male voice said, "Be careful, she is listening."

"At that point," Mariah said, "paranoia set in."

That night, on October 5, 1974, Mariah was again invited to bed to experience sexual passion. This time, her lovemaking with Reeves reached an unimaginable crescendo of physical passion. Mariah's body was set on fire inside; a passion so intense she thought she would explode of spontaneous combustion.

During this intense passion, however, she also became frightened. Mariah began to hear the voices in her head, this time screaming and chanting demonic sounds. In her mind, she saw realistic images of people dancing backward around an altar or table. Terrified and out of control, Mariah prayed. She recited the rosary in her mind. But the voices, sexual interaction, and imagery all continued to persist in frightening detail.

At the height of sexual passion, Mariah saw herself in another place, lying on a table. A white sheet was on the altar, and she was lying on it, nude. Fifteen or so persons, dressed in black robes, were dancing backwards around the table. They sang and chanted in demonic barks and screams. Mariah saw the same black haired, widow's peak hairline woman there in the group of dancing entities, as if the main character. She described the scene as a witches' black Sabbath "widdershins."

"I kept praying," Mariah continued, "and saying the rosary as I watched this horrifying scene in terror. Every time I said the rosary and prayed, the noise and chants would lessen. And if I lessened the prayers or dropped off to sleep, the sounds would increase."

As would be expected, Mariah didn't sleep well that night. She awoke at 5:00 a.m. the next morning, very shaken. The voices worsened with more and more dialogue, arguments, and accusations full of mimicking and mockery. Mariah could barely control herself. She felt as if there were other beings inside of her. With all of her strength, she struggled to phone the church. But she only reached a recorded message. Mariah recalled that morning:

"All the kids got up and saw me – a complete wreck – sitting at the table like I was insane. The kids got dressed by themselves and were terrified of me and left the house. I finally got a hold of a priest and begged, "I need help. Something terrible is wrong – I am demonically possessed!"

The priest asked, "Can you go and open the front door?" But Mariah was so out of control she could not even walk to the front door. It took everything she had just to stay on the phone until someone could come to get her. One of her children opened the door and left it unlocked.

When the priest arrived, he took the phone from Mariah's hand. Mariah later acknowledged that she looked crazy at the time. She told the priest that she had a demon. Within minutes, he took her to a local psychiatric center. Mariah was petrified that she might hurt her children, so she sent them to stay with their grandmother.

At the mental ward, Mariah was handed a paper to sign. She was so confused, however, that she was unable even to sign it. All she could muster was a long scribble across the page. She was given medication to calm her down. Still, she could hear voices of yelling, arguing, cursing, and mocking.

Her husband Clyde arrived, alerted to her situation from his place of work. He said demeaningly, "Mariah, for Gods sake, knock it off! There's nothing wrong with you!"

That was the last straw for Mariah. She let out a deathly

scream at him and then was out like a light. The medication kicked in. Mariah was hospitalized for thirteen days.

In hindsight Mariah admitted to Barbara, "Then I started to get well and I realized I had fallen in love with my kidnappers. I became a willing victim because I needed to have my needs fulfilled – and they were glad to do it for me. And what did they get from me? My mind and a lot of sexual energy."

Years after Mariah's love obsession with Jim Reeves and her recovery, she remained in contact with Barbara. Barbara asked Mariah, "Why do you think you had the sexual experience with this entity named Reeves?"

"This is a procedure they [the ETs turned into spirit guides] do with everyone," Mariah answered. "Anyone who is weakened by emotional trauma – that will be a part of the aliens so-called 'therapy.' They use the body on a sexual level after they've gained your trust. They say you are special and you don't need the human touch. Then you can become so intertwined with them they can supply all your sexual needs. It's like they want to keep you satisfied outside of interference with other humans. They use the sexual aspect almost like a weapon – a control factor."

Barbara asked Mariah to explain, "How exactly?"

"Whenever they allowed me to feel I was needed by someone else in another dimension or another factor besides the human factor (i.e., relationships) they would give, supply, and show me that I was somebody special. They needed me. They gave me not only the physical satisfaction but an emotional and spiritual application that they wanted me to do."

Barbara asked, "What about now Mariah? How can you look at this now that this experience is behind you?"

"After the experience I was freed of the yoke of their bondage – that this was a ploy to control us and to manipulate our thinking for them. The ego. They use the ego – like to make us feel special and unique as spokespersons, emissaries for these extraterrestrials. We have all these beautiful, benevolent deities at our beck and call. And they will supply us with what we want for very little in return. For example, they took my mind. They took my mind in exchange for curing my arthritis. That was a pretty stingy exchange, because I was pretty sick afterwards, emotionally sick.

"After the abduction and the automatic writing, I had information that no one else had that wasn't even in books. I later confirmed the information in ancient texts – and got a big ego on this one!"

Barbara asked Mariah, "Who was the group that was telepathically connecting to you?"

"Yes, these communications were connected to the abductions," Mariah replied. "They use a human-like image we can relate to because if we saw their true form it would give us night terrors! Whenever they dropped the façade of the human image they would become the reptilian image – just like on the TV show Babylon 5! For example, one time when I was alone I became aware of a physical interference with myself. I could see through the corner of my eyes two reptilian guards and a beautiful blonde human individual – who attempted to have sexual intercourse with me. Then when I said, "This is not what you look like" – its image would shimmer and diffuse and then showed a real image of a reptilian being. They do play on the ego, which is ok except for those with low self-esteem. Or for those who use drugs and alcohol so that they are left wide open for manipulation."

Barbara added, "Or for a woman who is sadly in need of love."

"Exactly," answered Mariah. "They will use that weapon against her. They'll make her feel like she is a true princess from another time; she is adored and worshipped. Then the downfall takes place and it's a crash, a traumatic experience. Like a beautiful glass vase that is dropped and crashes to the ground in a thousand pieces."

Barbara wondered out loud, "Why do you think all of this

could originate from the same Production Company?"

"In the beginning, I got healed, received high level information, spiritual knowledge and a great lover – Jim Reeves – a true obsession. Then I went through all that trauma. But after I healed and recovered I received inspirations on high spiritual wisdom and wrote a book called *Visions of Love and Wisdom*. It was almost as if I went through all of this horrible trauma and then was given inspiration and spiritual writings of love and wisdom. Maybe I was tested to see if I could succumb to the temptation of self-destruction.

"Everything started so subtly: the increase in intimate contact, the sexual relationship, and the obsession until it reached a crescendo. It really threw me over the edge. And of course I realize now that the lover was not the spirit of Jim Reeves, but the [reptilian] entity used that memory, façade and image of Reeves.

"I was pulled back from the ledge and I healed – kind of like in the Book of Job. They take you to the nth degree of your emotional capacity and see how you fare."

It is my opinion that these malevolent-acting entities, whether they are extraterrestrials, interdimensionals, demons, or non-human intelligent beings from another realm, all have one thing in common: the desire to create drama, chaos, and sexual energy for some kind of predatory feeding. And they do not play by rules of fairness or justice or even human reasoning. Deception is a hallmark of their predation. When taken to extremes, demonic possession can result. What saddens me is that when things get to this point, most religious clergy and new age healers cannot really help. The victim is left to figure it out alone.

In the next several chapters, I will provide red-flag warning signs and vulnerabilities to psychic vampirism. Luckily, most cases are not as severe as the last few case histories. But there are times when a good psychic self-defense tool kit is needed.

# Chapter 11

# Red Flags

A "red flag" is an internal warning system that goes off when you meet a dangerous person or situation. Many who experienced a paranormally-influenced love relationship realized their red flag warning signs only in hindsight. Some signs were subtle feelings of something "being not quite right," while others were more overt, such as nightmares and psychic warnings in the form of dreams or visions. Some people reported very physical warning sensations such as restlessness, stomach cramps, changes in appetite, jaw pain, and headaches. Others noticed mental or emotional symptoms such as anxiety or edginess.

All humans are born with a sensory response system which we commonly refer to as the "fight or flight" response. When confronted with danger, the autonomic nervous system releases adrenaline which causes the heart to beat faster in order to supply the muscles with more energy either to fight the threat or to escape it. In addition to rapid heartbeat, this causes physical symptoms of tightness in the stomach, hair standing on end, and sweating.

In some cases, responses can be reframed. When a child grows up associating verbal abuse and other dangers as normal, their "red flags" become repressed or ignored. Growing up in an alcoholic home where expression of negative feelings about the addiction and abuse are not allowed, or are met with punishment and denial, is one way this may happen, and may result in the development of unmet emotional needs. These may lie within a person like a black hole, or may be walled off through dissociation.

Adults who were abused or emotionally deprived as

children are less likely to respond to red flags. Yet, it is possible for them to recover their awareness of these physical reactions by paying close attention to their feelings and actively working to heal their traumas.

Doing it alone usually doesn't work. It is much more helpful to find a compassionate person to hear and understand us, someone who can help us become aware of our own blind spots. In the long run, isolation only creates more problems.

Regarding paranormal interference in our lives, the widespread lack of awareness is not only the result of trauma or some walled-off, unhealed psychic wound. It is usually more about our social conditioning or even, as I have found, outright censorship of such things as UFOs, extraterrestrials, mind control experimentation, ancient scriptures, or indigenous traditions which warn humanity about spiritual warfare.

Many, if not most, of the people who came to me with their "love bite" relationship were sensitive, intuitive individuals. Yet this did not always work in their favor when it came to red flag warning systems. I believe this indicates that we are dealing with something much more than a simple "toxic relationship" issue, easily explained by contemporary pop psychology. The Dark Side of Cupid is real. Open discussion about it is important. We need to take global responsibility for growing in spiritual discernment and stepping it up a notch in the emotional intelligence department!

We need to become aware of the specific red flags that often accompany the Dark Side of Cupid. These are indicators of an unseen interference factor. They may include paranormal activity, emotional tension, inability to consummate the love

> **We need to become aware of the specific red flags that often accompany the Dark Side of Cupid. These are indicators of an unseen interference factor.**

obsession, euphoric highs and crashing lows, mental changes like obsession, shifts in lifestyle and values, and energy drainage (either emotional or physical). These red flags are not necessarily in response to the love partner, but can be from the general atmosphere of the relationship itself, as if it were being arranged by an intelligent force behind the curtain. One must be mindful not to blame the partner when the Dark Side of Cupid hits, because there are other factors at work. Besides, blaming rarely helps, anyway.

More often than not, the red flags are recognized only in hindsight, after the love relationship gets going or even after it ends. The biggest obstacle to recognizing them in time is a simple lack of knowledge. Hopefully, this book will help.

*Red Flags in the Dark Side of Cupid Cases*

To summarize the main red flags noticed by my clients in the Dark Side of Cupid.

- Dreams of the partner before meeting them, suggesting something precognitive.
- Physical sensations in the solar plexus, genital, gut or other body areas, such as neck, heart, and between the shoulders.
- Astral sex visitations and/or telesthesia – sensing the energy body in a sexual way and very physically, as if another being were present but invisible.
- Strong psychic connection, even though you may not really love your partner.
- Powerful sexual passion and obsessive need to have sex, even though you don't love the partner or they don't love you and/or are abusive.
- Psychic responses and coincidences from either partner, like receiving a phone call or email from your partner the moment you think about cutting off the connection.
- A sense of emotional or physical draining.

- One partner becoming suddenly switched off emotionally or "psychically unplugged."
- Feelings of being watched, or being played like puppets in some drama-myth.
- Paranormal activity, third party "entity" visits or attacks, sudden dreams, visions and thoughts as if implanted.
- Obsessive thoughts that are not usual for either partner.
- Synchronicities, omens, and a feeling of being in a magical reality.

In the case of Wiz and Koral, Wiz experienced a twisting, contorting knot in his solar plexus area after having sex with Koral. As the relationship progressed, he became confused, exhausted, and depressed. Even after he and Koral broke up, Wiz continued to experience paranormal activity and unusual dreams, as if a dark force followed him around, sucking his energy. He reported this to me years after the relationship ended, and could feel a distinct energy-draining sensation between his shoulder blades, as if an entity had become attached to the back of his heart chakra area. This often happened in conjunction with sexual "astral attacks" in which he believed his sexual energy was being siphoned by predatory interdimensional entities.

In Maarit and Bjorn's story, Maarit noticed that she had reactions and decisions that were psychologically out of the ordinary for her, as she reacted more like a robot on automatic rather than in ways that were appropriate to the situation. Conditions seemed to be orchestrated so both of them were dependent on one another. Although Marit considered leaving, it never seemed like a viable option. Paranormal activity also occurred in their home.

Bjorn's behavior became cold and reckless, and took on abusive, jealous, and controlling overtones. When Maarit pursued spiritual practices like yoga and meditation, Bjorn dragged her down. In her case, the red flags were not apparent until after the relationship was fully established. These red flags were the unusual behaviors and reactions Maarit had around Bjorn in the beginning – the roller coaster emotional ride, paranormal activity, simultaneous engineered soul-melding experience, and the emotional manipulation of Bjorn. Luckily, this pattern shifted after Maarit took the responsibility to communicate and heal these issues with Bjorn, bringing these behaviors and their consequences to his attention. They are a unique couple in that they stayed together as a team, but it took great effort to create harmony, communication, and mutual support. This effort, however, did not stop the continual interference of their "Adjustment Bureau" watchers; Maarit and Bjorn just became more skilled at dealing with it.

In Max and Ishtar's case, Max sensed a presence around him as if he were being observed, and had the nagging sense from early on that Ishtar was being dishonest. On their first date, they experienced an unusual power outage which forced them to have dinner by candlelight, even though the rest of the neighborhood had no such problems. Max also experienced many physical red flag sensations, such as pain in his shoulders, lower back and throat, especially after he broke up with Ishtar. He even sensed more clearly the feeling of being watched by an invisible force which seemed to be connected to Ishtar. He also realized that many of his business and career plans were disrupted by his distraction, which resulted from the high drama of the relationship.

In Francine and Burt's case, Francine had two dreams of Burt before they became physically intimate, which described behaviors of his that she later realized to be true. Fearing exposure, she did not describe them in specifics, but they seemed to be a sixth sense warning about Burt's personality style. But Francine did not have a red flag warning about the invisible entity until after it attacked her after she had been with Burt. Like Max in his situation with Ishar, Francine felt

*Chapter 11: Red Flags*

this invisible entity watching as a third party, somehow connected to Burt.

Francine noticed herself feeling easily triggered emotionally. When Burt posted messages on his networking page regarding another woman, Francine felt invisible and rejected. She wondered if he deliberately created these statements to incite jealousy in her, but it had the opposite effect of pushing her away. Francine also noticed that Burt avoided eye contact with her. Even during the short time she and Burt were in communication with one another, she said it was one emotional high and low after another, not to mention the invisible entity attacking her, causing her stress and anxiety.

In the case of Michelle and Bernie, paranormal activity in the form of ghostly presences became apparent within a month of their relationship. Michelle noticed a difference between Bernie's outward social appearance and his real personality, in which he exhibited controlling and demeaning behaviors toward Michelle as well as a lack of empathy. As with Francine and Max, an invisible entity would visit and attack Michelle, leaving her stressed and physically exhausted, and indeed she experienced significant physical exhaustion and illness during her relationship with Bernie. Even when she knew she wanted to break up, she still found herself obsessed with wanting to be with him, which she knew was not characteristic for her. Like several others in my case histories, she experienced "astral sex" dreams which seemed real and energetically connected to Bernie. Later, when she pressed him for answers, Bernie admitted to his astral visitation abilities and hypnotic control over her.

In Nathan and Jezebel's relationship, Nathan became aware of a psychic link with Jezebel, and an ever-growing obsession with her – along with confusion. Nathan's friends noticed his mood and behavior shift from his formerly energetic, outgoing, and rational self, to one of seriousness and a compulsion to wear all-black, Goth-style clothing. Nathan also noticed, right after meeting Jezebel, sudden images and thoughts that seemed to enter his mind from elsewhere. These included visions of women being burned at the stake, as well as the taunting, ancient-looking, black hooded figures, suggestive of a past-life connection.

Nathan felt as if he were being emotionally whiplashed by Jezebel, constantly having to beg for forgiveness for some past-life sinful action and having to grovel for her attention and affection. He described her as a one-person demonic hierarchy. He also noticed how men were constantly following her around. By the midpoint of their relationship, Nathan started to develop an inner suspicion of the entire connection. As soon as his red flag warning system kicked in, he was able to end the relationship with surprising ease. The ease of this disconnection, combined with the emotional roller coaster and hypnotic nature of the drama, made Nathan question whether he had really been under some kind of spell.

In Kundra and Stan's love affair, Kundra was not initially attracted to Stan, but they shared a strong psychic bond. She later fell in love with him after Stan had engaged in magical rituals toward that end, definitely suggesting supernatural interference. They both experienced paranormal activity, as if the spirit guides that Stan channeled were playing the two of them in a myth of high drama, a magical mission to help free the world from evil dominion.

Kundra found herself so obsessively in love with Stan that being apart for even small periods of time was immensely painful, and she experienced an uncharacteristic willingness to be what he wanted. The emotional roller coaster dramas they fell into had the effect of fueling their love obsession. Her energy levels dropped so much that she developed chronic fatigue syndrome. Stan exhibited wildly jealous and controlling behaviors, to the point of apparent possession by the entities he channeled. At some point, Stan became suddenly emotionally switched off. During Kundra's affair with Stan, and even after they broke up, she still had vivid lovemaking dreams of him, as if they were still psychically connected.

In Gwen and Count Rokula's love bite relationship, there were several red flags in Gwen's experience: stomachaches, extreme fatigue, and numerous paranormal anomalies. Unfortunately, her red flags were not enough to counteract the obsessive, hypnotic feelings associated with the Dark Side of Cupid. The very powerful psychic connection had the effect of putting Gwen under a spell. And, like Amy and Thomas's connection, it was so tantrically intense that breaking up was extremely difficult, simply because something paranormal, hypnotic, and addictive was going on. A form of black magic?

In several of the cases, individuals reported feeling that their partner was some kind of conduit or host being overshadowed or temporarily possessed by another spirit. The more psychopathic behaviors caused their partners to feel rejection, then desire and yearning, hurt, shock, and feeling invisible and worthless. These behaviors seemed to be geared to pull the person back into the drama. For example, when Francine made a personal decision to disconnect from Burt, even while still thinking of him she would receive a call from him, as if he had a sixth sense. The psychic connections were too numerous to be considered coincidences, but seemed to be connected to another intelligent force pulling the strings to keep the couple engaged in an emotional roller coaster drama.

In these cases, the partners who appeared to have an attached entity exhibited narcissistic patterns of behavior. Some of these individuals were relatively high-profile in some way, or even religious clergy. I can't help but think of

> **In several of the cases, individuals reported feeling that their partner was some kind of conduit or host being overshadowed or temporarily possessed by another spirit.**

the "wolf in sheep's clothing" image here.

In James and Elizabeth's match, Elizabeth's initial reaction was a distinct solar plexus sensation, one that she recognized as both familiar and not quite right. But as her work friendship with James progressed into greater trust, she overrode this red flag. She experienced sexual dreams or what she recognized as "astral sex" with James before they outwardly became more intimately involved. Their psychic connection was strong, but the sexual dreams and conversations they had were not in keeping with James' evasive behavior regarding physical intimacy. Elizabeth confided that after speaking with James about the "astral sex," he did admit to having the ability to do this from a distance. The drama created by James's push-pull behaviors and emotional ping-pong confused Elizabeth so much that she consulted several psychics.

At the same time James pulled a tantrum at work, calling Elizabeth and other women misogynistic names, Elizabeth sensed a distinct physical sensation of a "chopping" pain in her neck. At that time, she felt a disconnection from James and she was able to psychically maintain her own space. Elizabeth then noticed that James no longer had the psychic hold over her, and his astral sex visits ceased. After the psychic disconnection, James wanted to apologize and reconnect with Elizabeth, but she refused. The ironic clincher in this drama was that after Elizabeth fully disconnected psychically from James, a flurry of other males started calling her, as if some supernatural intelligence wanted her to be linked up with other males that she was not attracted to. Simultaneously, her co-workers' attitudes turned cold. During the entire drama, Elizabeth had the gut feeling she and James were being watched and played like puppets in some bizarre, love-drama reality show.

These kinds of inexplicable coincidences are what some conspiracy researchers call the "reptilian-alien hive mind" of a contrived matrix reality manipulation. I know it sounds absolutely nuts, but so many have reported this in my work that this is beyond simple coincidence.

In Anna and Kaleb's affair, a red flag that Anna later recognized was that they seemed to have shared dreams as children. The psychic connection, telepathy, and telesthesia were new for Anna, and the bond she felt was greater than she ever experienced with anyone before. A telltale sign was the build up of intense passion and emotional connection, only to be severed all in one afternoon in a crashing low when Kaleb withdrew and decided not to pursue the relationship further.

Lucy and Pepe also shared an unusually strong psychic link, and Lucy felt that her initial dream of being on a bus that crashed and flipped over might have been a foreshadowing of how their relationship would develop—which certainly crashed and flopped in a big way. Lucy's observation of a dark, gargoyle-like entity overshadowing Pepe, especially during sex, was a red flag that this man was carrying around another demonic entity within him. Pepe's jealous and controlling behaviors, mental instability, and eerie sixth sense also warned Lucy that something about this relationship was askew. His sexual prowess and powerful psychic link drew Lucy in until she got tired of his game-playing and manipulative ways of controlling her.

Chapter 12

# Vulnerabilities to the Dark Side of Cupid

There are various qualities which can make one more vulnerable to being caught up in a Dark Side of Cupid relationship. Some of these, as noted on the questionnaires, are:

- Being financially or economically compromised.
- Being financially well off or having recently come into substantial money or assets.
- Being attracted to or in contact with powerful people, such as those within the entertainment or music, religious gurus, or icons.
- Involvement in a healing, caretaking, or nurturing profession such as social work, counseling, nursing, psychic intuitive work, or teaching.
- Involvement in research into the paranormal, spirituality, consciousness raising, conspiracy, and alternative media.
- Being shy, soft spoken, or lacking assertiveness.

In addition, I interviewed my clients for childhood trauma issues, addictions, and reports of familial paranormal activity, otherworldly visitations, and UFO sightings. I believe it is important to be mindful of possible windows of access, such as malevolent paranormal activity, in conjunction with relationships.

The term "window of access" is one way to describe an open doorway of vulnerability or boundary violation. It is a common term in contemporary Christian terminology denoting how a malevolent spirit can enter someone's life. For example, if a person experiences a psychic attack or demonic oppression, there are some doorways which might have allowed it to happen. Some of these include engaging in channeling, spiritual mediumship, Ouija boards, magical incantations, or staying in a haunted place known for paranormal activity. Other windows of access can be involvement in a sexual relationship with someone who has an overshadowing situation going on, whether this is an attached entity, a family "familiar spirit," or a demonic possession.

About seventy percent of my clients reporting a paranormally-influenced relationship were female. All respondents had a high interest in, or were researchers in, the alternative media, paranormal, spirituality, new age, or conspiracy fields. In a broader sense, all of these people were involved in the truth seeking, consciousness raising movement. They tended to think outside of the box. Seventy-one percent were financially compromised and economically burdened. Almost one-third were attracted to powerful people such as entertainers, professionals like famous authors, actors, or religious gurus. Seventy-one percent were in the caretaking, healing, or teaching professions, indicating a high compassion and empathy factor, as well as being highly intuitive or even psychic. Fifty-nine percent had assertiveness issues, and thirty percent had childhood trauma in their backgrounds with boundary issues, but surprisingly, not the majority of individuals as would be suspected with toxic relationships.[*]

*Summary of Basic Questionnaire Findings for Vulnerability*

Female. . . . . . . . . . . . . . . . . . . . . . . . . . . . . . . . . . . . . . . . . 70%
Alternative media, paranormal, etc.. . . . . . . . . . . . . . . . . . 99%
Financially compromised, economically burdened. . . . . . 70%
Attracted to Powerful People.. . . . . . . . . . . . . . . . . . . . . . . 30%

---

[*] Note: The three cases provided by Barbara Bartholic (Chapter 10) were not included in the questionnaire statistics, nor were Cecil and Rebecca (Chapter 9).

Caretaking, healing, teaching professions............ 71%
Childhood trauma............................... 30%
Alien visitations. ............................... 58%
Shyness, lack of assertiveness..................... 59%

Other vulnerability factors were also noteworthy. One was a general lack of awareness among respondents that such a thing could even happen. Another was the existence of an early trauma during childhood. Also, nearly sixty percent of the respondents said they had experienced alien visitations more than once in their lifetime.

*Vulnerability Factor # 1: Lack of Awareness*

The single largest vulnerability factor in my opinion is lack of awareness that this kind of relationship could happen. Even among exceptionally aware individuals who engaged in positive healing, higher awareness modalities, and the alternative media, people were deceived and shocked when they were hit over the head by the Dark Side of Cupid. All my clients who reported a Dark Side of Cupid relationship were unaware of its possibility before it happened to them.

*Vulnerability # 2: Early Childhood Trauma*

These are observations I have made over the years while counseling people who have suffered trauma and abuse in particular. Lucy, Francine, Maarit, Michelle, and Gwen all experienced trauma during their childhoods, which represents about 30% of respondents. They also exhibited a natural psychic ability, but oddly enough this sixth sense didn't help them avert toxic relationships. I believe that these earlier childhood traumas, and their inability to perceive the red flags, created a window of access for them to attract the more sociopathic partners and form relationships with them.

Red flags are the signals which tell you that there is danger nearby. These factors are often unconscious and body oriented, such as rapid heartbeat, a knot in the stomach, neck pain, anxiety, nightmares, or more subtle feelings to avoid someone or even avert eye contact.

When we are present and heart-centered we can more easily connect with our feelings. The problem of lack of awareness arises when we habitually disconnect from our feelings for the sake of survival, and to avoid painful emotions. Those who have been raised in unhealthy environments, such as alcoholic homes, or homes where there had been abuse (emotional, physical, or sexual), cults, or military combat training, are the most vulnerable to being disconnected from their feelings. In order for these individuals to reconnect to their heart, and hence their feelings, they must be willing to re-integrate via counseling, healing, and recovery work. Doing it alone doesn't work. Why? Because we all have blind spots and it takes others who are more aware, present, and compassionate to help us through these blind alleys of the self.

A large part of reconnecting to one's feelings is to pause daily to engage in self-reflection, when you can become aware of habituated and unconscious behaviors that dissociate you from being fully present. Compulsions, addictions, distractions, and difficulty being intimate with others on emotional levels are symptoms of hidden pain in the heart.

Normally, most people want to avoid painful, uncomfortable feelings, especially if it affects their ability to function in a particular environment. But when feelings are shoved into the recesses of one's being for too long, one can become numb and unaware on emotional levels. This numbness can take away the ability to feel joy and love on deeper levels, and of course it is unfulfilling for others if you are in a relationship with them. The fear factor tends to keep many people away from facing uncomfortable feelings. Simple things like fear of rejection and confrontation can result in lack of assertiveness and shyness, which is one of the vulnerability issues noted. If we cannot confront toxic people and their behaviors, we tend to become their victims.

Being present with uncomfortable feelings takes courage and patience. It is best done when you are alone or with a compassionate friend or counselor who can help draw out your feelings in a safe, nurturing environment.

Without therapeutic help, the person with repressed trauma and pain will most likely repeat dysfunctional relationship patterns, unless they heal from the original issues. Healing involves grieving the losses at some point, which will be more fully explored in the chapter on grieving and bereavement.

In a nutshell, without healing and awareness, the black holes in one's emotional being will create windows of vulnerability. The red flags possessed by fully aware, integrated, emotionally present people won't be there for you. That puts you at a disadvantage to being pierced by the arrows of the Dark Side of Cupid.

*Vulnerability # 3: Attraction to or by Famous Powerful People or Gurus*

In several of these stories, as well as a number of unpublished cases I've consulted, people reported a toxic relationship with partners who were powerful people. These were entertainers, religious gurus, or public figures who had a certain amount of power, money, or both. In the published cases, 29% were of this category. Cult leaders and religious gurus were big on the list of being a manipulative narcissist or psychopath, hosting some type of attached entity. The most lethal combination in terms of the Dark Side of Cupid were those with traumatic childhoods later being matched up with a sociopathic guru for a partner. Such combinations displayed what I call the third-party entity situation.

The issue here isn't really money, but power. Many types of psychopathic people are attracted to power and the control they can have over others. I believe sociopathy and narcissism are directly linked to evil, or at least evil behaviors. (Unless the sociopath heals, integrates, and develops true empathy, but don't hold your breath!) I believe sociopathy attracts

> **In a nutshell, without healing and awareness, the black holes in one's emotional being will create windows of vulnerability.**

a type of paranormal viral factor, such as demons. These demons may influence or even host the sociopath or psychopath, who then feeds off of his or her victim emotionally, like a psychic vampire. Based on my studies, I believe these demonic entities can interfere with and orchestrate relationships.

*Vulnerability # 4: Being Poor*

Having little money and being economically compromised can cause problems and self-esteem issues that ultimately affect relationships. Seventy-one percent of my respondents had money issues. Being financially dependent will also put people – especially women – into bad situations, or keep them in bad relationships longer than they would put up with if they had the money to escape the pit of poverty and abuse.

In Nathan and Jezebel's story, economic hardship was an issue, but this was not the overriding factor that was the major vulnerability. In Nathan's case, he believed the culprit was his alternative media research and whistle blowing.

*Vulnerability # 5: Engagement in Alternative Media, Research, Conspiracy, and Paranormal & Spirituality*

All but one respondent who filled out my Dark Side of Cupid questionnaire was a follower of alternative media, paranormal, conspiracy, and/or spirituality interests. These were individuals who were actively engaged in becoming aware of what is going on in the world and cosmos, including higher consciousness explorations. These people tended to do a lot of internet research and radio talk show involvement, and had interests in spirituality and the paranormal. All persons were intelligent, "outside-the-box" thinkers, who challenged the status quo of mainstream media, education, politics, and religion. Some were whistleblowers. Many of them had psychic abilities and a greater awareness on social and esoteric levels.

One may ask, how can this be a vulnerability factor? If lack of awareness were a major vulnerability factor why would aware people be so vulnerable? In a later chapter I will address this apparent paradox.

*Vulnerability # 6: Involvement in Caretaking and Nurturing Professions*

Over two-thirds of the Dark Side of Cupid cases involved people in careers such as teaching, counseling, nursing, and psychic intuitive work. These individuals have a tendency for a high empathy factor, and are more giving in nature. As a result, they sometimes have greater difficulty setting firmer boundaries with "user and taker" partners, friends, and co-workers. According to Sandra L. Brown, author of *How to spot a Dangerous Man* and founder for The Institute for Relational Harm Reduction and Public Psychopathy Education, psychopaths are prone to targeting these kinds of people.[*] I wholeheartedly agree.

*Vulnerability # 7: Shyness or Lack of Assertiveness*

Fifty-nine percent of the respondents reported that they were shy and had assertiveness issues. Among them were the thirty percent who had former abuse issues, and were involved with the more lethal, narcissistic partners who were influenced

---

[*] See "Professionals in the Helping Industries and Their Personal Pathological Relationships." http://saferelationshipsmagazine.com/professionals-in-the-helping-industries-and-their-personal-pathological-relationships-2

by non-human entities. Shyness often goes hand in hand with a lack of boundaries. These people tend to get walked on before they stand up for themselves or break off the relationship. The notable thing here, too, is that once a person is hooked up with a pathological, narcissistic type of partner, even using assertive, compassionate, communication skills may not be effective. Abusers and manipulators usually do not respond to "fair play" in relationships. Psychopaths deceive, manipulate, and control by nature. They will do what they can, and get away with what they can. They lack empathy.

In essence, shy people and those who have boundary issues have greater difficulties in relationships if they get into partnerships with controlling, manipulative people because simple communication and assertiveness skills, even when strategically applied, fail. This is not necessarily because of their lack of skill, but because of their tendency to get into dysfunctional relationships with partners who are users and takers. They are essentially "too nice" and tend to be doormats. Hence they will attract psychopaths if they are not careful. Often, once a shy person learns new skills, their old relationships will fall away simply because they were in a relationship with a person who did not play fair in the first place, and most likely never will – if that person was an abuser.

The reason I am making a point of this is because those who have gone through trauma, and hence have poor boundaries, are more likely to get stuck in bad relationships with controlling and manipulative partners. Those who have been formerly abused do not fully trust their feelings and perceptions, and this is why their red flag warning systems are not fully operable, or they do not listen to them as attentively as they should. Only after they commit to counseling, healing, and recovery, do they shift gears and start attracting more healthy partners.

However, communication skills alone do not guarantee that a person will be treated with respect and fairness. Nor will more assertive people necessarily instinctively deflect psychopaths and abusers. It is important to recognize that true psychopaths are expert deceivers and manipulators, even with people who have no former abuse history or assertiveness issues. Trusting your instincts is a better skill to develop. It all goes back to awareness, emotional intelligence, and self-respect.

Blaming the victim is a prevailing trend today, especially in New Age circles where the common mantra is: "You create your own reality." If you ever encounter a true psychopath or become involved in a relationship with one, that mantra will be of no use to you.

And if the Dark Side of Cupid ever hits you with a lover who is a narcissist, or host to a non-human entity, your worldview may be shattered.

Chapter 13

# Psychological Intervention and Communication Strategies

The majority of those who experienced being struck by the Dark Side of Cupid broke off the love relationship. Even though the lover appeared to be the soul mate due to the magical and extraordinary circumstances, it turned out differently, and for the majority of them, badly. Only one couple, Maarit and Bjorn, maintained the relationship, and that was only after much hard work and with full awareness of the "otherworldly influence" involved. Perhaps more of these matches could have been saved had the couples employed extreme measures of patience, compassionate communication skills, mutual negotiation, and awareness-enhancing practices such as meditation. However, considering the circumstances, this is not realistic, and only those who exhibit heroic measures are likely to save a Dark Side of Cupid relationship.

A more realistic approach is to have an intervention strategy for the relationship once it exhibits signs of being out of control. When I say out of control, I mean extraordinarily difficult or unusual situations that keep the couple from being able to consummate the relationship, or uncomfortable feelings like obsessive longing, yearning, and pain of separation keeping either partner wrung out emotionally and physically. Other problems such as the ecstatic highs, crashing lows, or dealing with an abusive, psychopathic emotional vampire partner are a bit more challenging to deal with. Paranormal activity is also an issue, and appears to be fueled by higher degrees of negative emotional drama.

Intervention strategies involve recognition, management, and healing of the trauma-drama love affair. This chapter will address the first two factors, recognition and management of the Dark Side of Cupid relationship. Ultimately, a proactive approach of prevention is desirable and is best accomplished through the creation of community education and support.

*Recognition*

Recognition of being hit by the Dark Side of Cupid involves a range of emotional perception. Sensitivity to one's own feelings will make it easier to relate to others with understanding. The degree to which we are able to be present with our own emotions is the degree in which we can be aware and present to other's emotions. But with the Dark Side of Cupid, we encounter another issue that can even be problematic for emotionally intelligent, empathic individuals. This is the paranormal-supernatural factor, involving outright psychopathic emotional vampires and what I believe to be spiritual warfare. But first, let us address emotional awareness.

*Emotional Awareness*

Emotional awareness seems to be a simple, common sense thing. In general, women are more sensitive to emotions and express them verbally more openly than men. Men tend to be more rational and body oriented, but they feel emotions too, although they may express them differently. Women are more likely to want to talk about relationships and engage in verbal communication. Because women tend to be more receptive and sensitive then men, more of them are psychic, as well. This sixth sense (what some call women's intuition) can be very useful in recognizing characteristics and patterns in relationships, as well as subtle nuances which may be red flags for toxic relationships.

How can we increase our emotional intelligence and awareness?

Emotional Intelligence, or EI, describes an ability or capacity to perceive, assess, and manage the emotions of one's self and of others. Another, more thorough definition of

## Chapter 13: Psychological Intervention and Communication Strategies

emotional intelligence is discussed by John Meyers and contributors on his web site dedicated to emotional intelligence:

> "Emotional intelligence refers to an ability to recognize the meanings of emotion and their relationships, and to reason and problem-solve on the basis of them. Emotional intelligence is involved in the capacity to perceive emotions, assimilate emotion-related feelings, understand the information of those emotions, and manage them."
>
> *Emotion*
>
> In this model, emotion refers to a feeling state (including physiological responses and cognitions) that conveys information about relationships. For example, happiness is a feeling state that also conveys information about relationships–typically, that one would like to join with others. Similarly, fear is a feeling state that corresponds to a relationship – the urge to flee others." *

When discussing emotional intelligence, the "intelligence" component refers to the ability to apply reason to factual information. The "emotional" component is how we interact with others based on this information. An emotionally intelligent person uses both qualities in balance.

Calming the mind is the first step to open one up to greater degrees of awareness. This can be accomplished through taking time to be alone, to be still and present with oneself. One of the most common forms of meditation is focusing on the breath in order to calm the mind, but other variations include repeating a mantra to focus the mind, or meditating while walking.

Another method is to tune into the body by scanning oneself very slowly from head to foot, taking special care to

---

*http://www.unh.edu/emotional_intelligence/ei%20What%20is%20EI/ei%20definition.htm

notice sensations such as tightness, heaviness, pain, or numbness. This is a very effective method for tuning into one's emotions on a subtle level, because oftentimes we hold tension and pain in our bodies unconsciously. Our bodies will pick up the perception first, as was mentioned in the chapter on Red Flags. Examples of bodily sensations are sudden pain in the neck, stomach tightening, shoulder, neck, jaw tension, or heat in some areas. Physical symptoms like nausea, anxiety, sweating, heart racing, and frequent nightmares are also clues that there are emotions which need our attention, or warning signs of danger. Body language and posture is important because chronic negative emotions will manifest in our musculature. Positive emotions and confidence will also show up in our posture.

A great way of enhancing the body-mind connection – and hence, greater awareness of our emotions – is through an exercise program like tai-chi, yoga, and walking meditations.

Counseling, therapy, and support groups are excellent ways to explore one's feelings and the needs that are beneath those feelings. It is important to recognize unconscious and reactive ways we avoid our own emotional pain and submerged issues, which still carry a negative charge. These affect how we perceive and interact with the world. Some schools of thought refer to these basic patterns as psychological defenses that show up in our personality patterns.

Developing emotional awareness and intelligence means being willing to be present with our feelings and needs, respecting others and engaging in mindfulness practices. Tracking our behavior patterns, such as compulsions, addictions, and things that "trigger" us emotionally, is essential to expanding our awareness. It's part of raising our consciousness and evolving as human beings, and I believe it is essential for peace and harmony on this planet. We cannot manage, change, or heal from our issues until we acknowledge that the issues are there. This requires a steadfast intention on awareness and positive change, and we must take personal responsibility for our own healing and growth.

## Managing and Coping Methods

Once that we've recognized there is a problem with the Dark Side of Cupid relationship, we can develop ways to manage our frustrations. Even with various mindfulness, meditation, or body-mind exercise programs, we still can be left with powerful emotional fallout and possibly paranormal activity, not to mention having to deal with emotional vampires and psychopathic people in some cases. As our first line of defense, let's talk about compassionate communication skills.

## Compassionate Communication Skills

My first introduction to compassionate communication was through a coach and educator in Asheville, NC, USA named Jerry Donoghue. His compassionate communication training program employs the basic methods of Marshall Rosenberg, Ph.D., also known as Nonviolent Communication (NVC).[*] What I value about this form of communication is that it cuts through the chase of round-about psychobabble and complicated psychoanalysis, and forces us to be present with basic human feelings and the needs that lie at the core of those feelings. It creates a flow between oneself and others based on a mutual giving from the heart. Rosenberg describes it this way:

> "NVC guides us in reframing how we express ourselves and hear others. Instead of being habitual, automatic reactions, our words become conscious responses based firmly on awareness of what we are perceiving, feeling and wanting. We are led to express ourselves with honesty and clarity, while simulta-

---

[*] http://www.ashevilleccc.com

neously paying others a respectful and empathic attention. In any exchange, we come to hear our own deeper needs and those of others. NVC trains us to observe carefully, and to be able to specify behaviors and conditions that are affecting us. We learn to identify and clearly articulate what we are concretely wanting in a given situation. The form is simple, yet powerfully transformative.

As NVC replaces our old patterns of defending, withdrawing or attacking in the face of judgment and criticism, we come to perceive ourselves and others, as well as our intentions and relationships, in a new light. Resistance, defensiveness, and violent reactions are minimized. When we focus on clarifying what is being observed, felt and needed rather than on diagnosing and judging, we discover the depth of our own compassion." *

In a nutshell, NVC is a way to connect with each other and ourselves from the heart and focuses our awareness on four basic areas: what we are observing, feeling, and needing, and what we request to allow those needs to be met. To do so, we must be good listeners. We must be willing to be present enough to reflect back what the other is saying, so that they feel heard, understood, and respected.

In our patriarchal culture, in which logic and rationality is valued above feelings, we naturally will have difficulty identifying and expressing feelings. The key here is being able to express one's observations, perceptions, feelings, and needs in a way that will be more easily received. This means communicating in a way where the person doesn't feel judged, blamed, or manipulated. According to Rosenberg, life-alienating ways of communication originate from, and support, hierarchical or domination societies. I couldn't agree more! This is much like

---

\* Marshall Rosenberg, *Nonviolent Communication: A Language of Life*, Puddle Dancer Press, (2005), p. 3.

*Chapter 13: Psychological Intervention and Communication Strategies*

> **When we are truly in contact with our feelings and needs, we humans no longer make good slaves.**

our culture, in which large populations are controlled by a minority of elite, who benefit from educating (or mind controlling) the masses to encourage a slave-like hive mentality. In these societies, we get a lot of language of wrongness, and good-bad moralistic judgments where people are essentially trained to look outside of themselves to "authorities" for definitions of right, wrong, good, and bad, as well as "God."

But when we are truly in contact with our feelings and needs, we humans no longer make good slaves. When we are connected and live fully from our hearts, we will have a natural outflowing of compassion. In this sense, emotional intelligence and liberation from slave mentality means being able to state clearly what we feel and need in a way that communicates we are equally concerned that the needs of others be fulfilled.

*Compassionate Communication in Practice*

To put compassionate communication into practice in our relationships, think of it as using the four basics: observation, feelings, needs, and requests. For example, let's say your partner did or said something that triggered some uncomfortable feelings. In Chapter 6, Nathan's observation of Jezebel seemed to indicate that she had a romantic attraction for him because of their shared strong psychic connection, possible past life memories, and the fact that Jezebel asked him, "Where have you been all my life?" He also started feeling emotionally whiplashed because Jezebel avoided any physical intimacy, and entertained the past life myth that Nathan did horrible things like burning her and others at the stake. This left him with an inferred sense of guilt, as if he needed to beg for her forgiveness and grovel for her attention. When he did get close

*The Dark Side of Cupid*

to her, she felt cold as ice. To top it off, Jezebel made a casual comment to Nathan about her "having a boyfriend" with complete insensitivity, considering Nathan's romantic feelings for her. How might Nathan have communicated some of his observations, feelings, needs, and a request?

Let's start with Nathan's feeling "emotionally whiplashed" when Jezebel avoided intimacy, complicated by the guilt induced by past life memories of Nathan being "the bad guy." Nathan could perhaps have said,

"Jezebel, I felt a bit confused and hurt when you avoided closeness with me because I really wanted to express and explore my feelings of attraction and deep connection with you. When you asked me after we first met, "Where have you been all my life?" I thought you experienced a strong connection with me too, plus all the esoteric interests we shared and those powerful synchronicities. It felt meaningful to me, and I thought to you too. Would you be willing to share with me honestly how you are feeling about all of this, and what you want from me?"

This may seem a bit wordy, but can be broken up in a way in which an observation, feeling, need, and request are given. It also offers reasons why Nathan understands and perceives the situation the way he does. Let's break it down:

*Observation:* When you avoided closeness with me.

*Feeling:* Confused and hurt.

*Need:* Express and explore my feelings of attraction and deep connection.

*Request:* Would you be willing to share with me honestly how you are feeling about all of this and what you want from me?

Nathan's request is for simple honesty for Jezebel to be clear about what she is feeling and what she wants from him. His perception indicates that he is getting mixed messages from her. We don't know how she would respond here, but by leaving it open-ended and as non-blaming as possible, we make

*Chapter 13: Psychological Intervention and Communication Strategies*

it easier for her to respond.

Here we haven't even addressed other issues such as Nathan's feeling like he's being judged as the bad guy, with inferences of guilt and blame about alleged, evil past life deeds, not to mention his shock and hurt when Jezebel told him casually and insensitively that she already had a boyfriend. Perhaps Jezebel got scared and didn't want to pursue the relationship further. But instead of being forthright and honest, it appears she made indirect comments to push Nathan away when he wanted to get close. The past life memories are another issue, which only complicated matters in ways that made Nathan feel as though he were being branded indirectly as "the bad guy." If Nathan wanted to communicate more of what he was feeling and needing, he could share more, such as:

"Jezebel, when you shared with me your beliefs of our past life connection, I felt angry and embarrassed because I need to be respected for who I am now, and that I matter to you. Then when you announced to me so casually that you had a boyfriend, I felt shocked and resentful because I really wanted some consideration and a mutual connection with you."

At this point in the relationship a request was not in order, because at that point Nathan had decided to break up. It was beyond repair and obvious to him that Jezebel had no respect for him, and the wish for a closer connection was not mutual.

Broken down into the observation, feeling, needs:

*Observation:* When you shared with me your beliefs of our past life connection, AND when you announced to me so casually that you had a boyfriend.

*Feeling:* angry and embarrassed, AND shocked and resentful.

*Need:* respected for who I am now and that I matter to you AND consideration and a mutual connection with you.

*Other NVC Examples*

I'd like to share some simple examples of complaints I've

heard over the years from people I've counseled. More often than not, when we are trying to express ourselves we may do so with words that are not true feeling words, so that the communication comes across as a criticism or as if the person is being blamed or judged.    For example:

*Scenario One: Using a non-feeling word that comes across in a critical way*

When my husband responded to me condescendingly, "There are of a lot other people in the world who have worse suffering," after I complained about being exhausted from a long day of housework and child care, I felt minimized and unimportant.

NVC method: "I felt disappointed and frustrated because I needed acknowledgment and appreciation for the things I do, when I'd rather be doing something else."

*Scenario Two: Using a non-feeling word.*

"When my wife responded to me with inattentive silence after I started a conversation with her, I felt invisible."

Using NVC: "When my wife did not respond to my attempts at conversation, I felt lonely and angry because I wanted inclusion and connection with her."

*Scenario Three: Judgmental example.*

"When you didn't respond to my email about a disturbing incident that happened to me, after I had responded to many of your concerns, I felt invalidated and discounted compared to all of your 'more important life issues.'"

NVC: "When you didn't respond to my email about the disturbing incident that happened to me, after I had replied to numerous of your emails, I felt disappointed and hurt because I wanted some support and more mutuality in our friendship."

Let's take another story from the Dark Side of Cupid, that of Lucy and Pepe.

Lucy started having nightmares and "astral attacks" soon

*Chapter 13: Psychological Intervention and Communication Strategies*

after having sex with Pepe. She also noticed that Pepe started exhibiting jealousy and control issues, making judgmental comments about how she dressed, inferring that her clothes were too skimpy and showed too much skin. Lucy's sixth sense picked up that Pepe harbored a dark, menacing, gargoyle-like entity within him, and the times when she observed this entity coincided with Pepe's angry outbursts and jealous behaviors. For Lucy, it was important to be able to share her sixth sense perceptions, and to feel understood about her concerns of observing something anomalous happening around Pepe and their relationship. Her gut instinct and red flags were telling her that her nightmares and his angry, controlling, jealous behaviors and mood swings were somehow connected to the demonic entity that overshadowed him. At the same time, Lucy felt an incredible connection to Pepe and enjoyed great sex with him.

Pepe started feeling insecure that Lucy was drawing too much male attention with her clothing choices. When Lucy started to pull away because of his controlling, jealous criticisms, Pepe became even more manipulative, jealous, and controlling. How might Lucy have intervened in communicating her concerns to Pepe, and how might he communicate to her his insecurities?

For example:

Lucy: "Pepe, when you told me to change my blouse the other day because I showed too much skin, I felt hurt and pressured because I value autonomy in my own dress choices and comfort in this hot weather. If this really bothers you, would you be willing to take me clothes shopping for some summer clothes?"

*Let's break it down into:*

*Observation:* when you told me to change my blouse the other day because I showed too much skin.

*Feeling:* hurt and pressured.

*Need:* autonomy in my own dress choices, and comfort.

*Request:* would you be willing to take me clothes shopping for some summer clothes

How might Pepe share his concerns about Lucy's clothing choices?

Pepe: "When I saw you wearing that skimpy blouse the other day in public, I felt scared because I am concerned about your safety from other men and sexual predators. Next time we are out in public would you be willing to wear something less skimpy?

*Breakdown:*

*Observation:* When I saw you wearing that skimpy blouse the other day in public

*Feeling:* scared

*Need:* concern for safety

*Request:* would you be willing to wear something less skimpy

Now, let us address some of the more disturbing issues and observations that Lucy had concerning Pepe's "overshadowing attached entity" and coincidental controlling, jealous and angry behaviors, not to mention the sinking feeling that this relationship has been somehow orchestrated. Lucy could have phrased her feelings, needs, and observation to Pepe something like this.

Lucy: Pepe, I need to share some feelings I've had about things that concern us. First off, I want to say that I've never experienced such a powerful connection with anyone, and our sex life is absolutely great. But the other night – and several times afterwards, I have noticed – psychically – a large, dark entity overshadowing you. I also started to have nightmares about this demonic entity ever since the first time we had sex. This scares me. I also noticed that the same times that I saw this entity around and overshadowing you, you had mood swings and became controlling, angry and possessive. I'm having mixed feelings here because while I really enjoy our sexual relationship and incredible connection, I'm also scared

*Chapter 13: Psychological Intervention and Communication Strategies*

and frustrated that this entity overshadowing you is influencing your moods. I'm starting to become concerned for my safety and freedom in this relationship. It almost seems as if our relationship is being somehow manipulated through this entity or something I can't quite explain.

In essence, Lucy expresses a need to be heard and understood regarding her feelings about her observations. She knows it may be hard for him to hear, so she prefaces her "bad news" with the good news about how she's experienced a powerful connection and good sex with him.

Lucy shares several observations connecting the demonic entity she sees overshadowing Pepe with his mood swings and controlling behavior. She states she has mixed feelings, positive ones with regards to the incredible connection and sex, but negative ones, like fear for her safety and lack of autonomy with Pepe. She also expressed confusion about whether these incidents are somehow manipulated through this demonic entity. What Lucy needs is safety, understanding, and autonomy. At some point she may want some empathy from Pepe by requesting a reflection of what he heard her say. But this would take a counseling session, with communication broken down in smaller steps in a safe environment.

If Lucy shares this much in one breath, Pepe may become overwhelmed and defensive. At the same time, Lucy really needs to be heard and understood, to feel safe and to establish clear boundaries for her own autonomy. In fact, if Pepe's behaviors do not change, she may have to become much more assertive, set firmer boundaries, or break up altogether. Of course, one has to wonder if the relationship is really being complicated by the demonic entity that Lucy has observed numerous times by now.

It turned out that Lucy and Pepe broke up several times, each dating others in between. But when they reconciled and re-established their relationship, Lucy noticed Pepe becoming even more jealous, and discovered later that he threatened violence against one of the men she casually dated. Pepe also manipulated the situation by threatening to commit suicide when Lucy wanted to break it off for good. Pepe became a danger to himself and others with these threats.

This is when another intervention strategy must be carried out. Compassionate communication skills are great, but when we are dealing with psychopaths or demonically-influenced individuals, we must be much more firm in setting boundaries which include consequences if they do not comply.

It turned out in Lucy's case that she and her new boyfriend, Alejandro, called his bluff, and Pepe walked away with his tail between his legs. But I would not suggest testing or escalating any form of violence or threats of suicide. At this point in the relationship, it was best for Lucy to leave for good. And she did.

One thing I'd like to stress here is that in cases where there is obviously a large problem, where things just feel orchestrated beyond the norm and when one person exhibits abuse, psychopathy, or narcissism, it may be better to establish clear safe boundaries first. Then, if boundaries are not respected, sever ties quickly. When these things occur, it is a reminder and wake up call that with the Dark Side of Cupid, these are not normal, easily explained relationship difficulties or differences between men and women. Interference by the paranormal requires an extra degree of awareness, diligence, and spiritual strength.

In our next chapter we will explore various paranormal intervention strategies, if the first line of defense with psychological communication skills is not effective.

Chapter 14

# Paranormal Intervention Strategies

In this chapter I will discuss paranormal intervention strategies and proactive measures we can take to help us become more resilient against the effects of the Dark Side of Cupid. These strategies are necessary because simple psychological methods alone are inadequate. A spiritual answer is needed, because we are dealing with a complex relationship problem that borders on a form of spiritual warfare and emotional energy vampirism.

It is essential to raise our awareness of emotional and subtle energy. Then we must be open to explore emotional healing. Once we can be clear about what our feelings and needs are, we then can learn how to establish and maintain clear boundaries within our relationships. Ultimately spiritual purification and empowerment practices can help in proactively enhancing our emotional intelligence and spiritual power.

The line of defense for the Dark Side of Cupid is multifaceted, comprising the following elements:

*Education and Awareness – The Recognition Factor*
- Compassionate Communication Skills and Boundary Setting
- Emotional Processing and Clearing
- Spiritual Cleansing
- Proactive Spiritual Empowerment

In a later chapter we will deal with the grieving issues of losing a lover.

In order to deal with paranormal situations, one must first understand what is happening. Before we can strategize here, we need to say something about what at least half of the Dark Side of Cupid experiencers observed, which was a third-party entity.

## Third Party Entity Interference

In at least half of my case histories, and many unpublished cases I have encountered over the years, one partner reported that they observed a third-party entity either overshadowing, influencing, or outright possessing the other partner. Sometimes this third-party entity seemed to orchestrate and influence the relationship to create unnecessary drama and emotional chaos. In this type of relationship, simple compassionate communication skills may be inadequate. This is not to marginalize the effectiveness of such dialogue; in fact, I encourage the use of it to diffuse any misunderstandings that could potentially lead to abuse and violence. However, it is not always enough to deal with manipulation by an outside entity.

## Perceptual Variations

After two decades of researching anomalous trauma, and more recently what I call love bite relationships, I have concluded that the paranormal factor is very real and we must deal with it. The problem with paranormal complications lies in the fact that not all individuals can perceive what is happening on more subtle levels of reality – let alone understand it. Even in "regular" relationships we have misunderstandings, where one partner perceives something of which the other is unaware, and this may become a flashpoint of contention. There are varying degrees of differences in perception, even day to day, and that is normal to deal with.

What I'm talking about are widely divergent perceptions because one individual is essentially unaware of their own internal process, emotional well-being, and spiritual identity. In the Dark Side of Cupid, perceptual variations are exacerbated because, for the majority of cases, one partner was more aware than the other when it came to seeing behind the facade of physical reality.

There are two issues here that need addressing.
- One partner has a higher degree of awareness on subtle and emotional levels of reality, and/or both partners disagree on what they are perceiving in situations that cause distress.
- An independent "third party entity," aka "Cupid," demonic entities, or other paranormal viral factors, are interfering with the relationship to cause emotional trauma and suffering.

Perceptual variations between two partners – and disagreements thereof – are one thing, but an assault on consciousness through deliberate orchestration of disharmonious love relationships is entirely a different matter. And this is the infectious culprit I believe we are dealing with. This is where paranormal intervention is needed. Let me explain my hypothesis simply.

There is an assault on the raising of human consciousness and harmonious love relationships by a viral "paranormal factor" I have defined as The Dark Side of Cupid. Some may call it demonic, alien, artificial intelligence, or the ancient, mythical Cupid playing games.

Why do I believe this? Because nearly all of my respondents who reported a Dark Side of Cupid relationship were actively involved in research of

> **Is this an ancient war on the attempt to raise humanity's consciousness above the slave mentality?**

alternative media, spirituality, and/or higher consciousness study. Some had reported extraterrestrial encounters and ghostly visitations. All were dissatisfied with what the mainstream media, educational system, orthodox religion, or politics told them. Why? Because their experiences and explorations of what was going on in their lives and in the world was not the same reality as what they were being told by mainstream establishment sources and global elite policy makers. The people who experienced the Dark Side of Cupid were not good little slaves with a hive mind. In my opinion, they were able to perceive things outside the box, and were actively engaged in activities which expand and redefine the outmoded herd mentality.

I had to ask myself: Is this an ancient war on the attempt to raise humanity's consciousness above the slave mentality? Spiritual warfare? Or is this simply a paranormal manifestation of parasitic soul-energy vampirism?

Maybe both. The only way we can approach this dilemma is to raise our own awareness, to recognize that there is a problem so we can start dealing with it, and heal from it. We must set forth intervention strategies and proactive measures to create the relationships we want that will not feed the Dark Side of Cupid.

I am reminded of a mother's wisdom: All peace in the world starts at the core of our love relationships and family. We must start here.

*A Viral Metaphor*

I like to view the Dark Side of Cupid as an alien virus, a sociopathic parasite if you will. It is, I believe, the greatest test of human emotional and spiritual strength. It masquerades as all kinds of other diseases and can even look like the cure. In small doses, it won't be as noticeable and may even add some spice to the relationship. But in larger doses, it eventually kills the host, the love relationship itself.

Paranormal intervention number one is to strengthen our own emotional and spiritual immune systems so that we are resistant to the virus. These strategies are the basic methods already discussed, such as meditation, body-mind exercises, compassionate communication skills, and healthy living.

Paranormal intervention number two is to remove the

parasite-virus that is infecting the love relationship.

Our hearts, minds, and souls need cleansing on a regular basis. Even the most astute and spiritually dedicated people can be on the Dark Side of Cupid's hit list. In fact, I believe that people who are directed by a higher consciousness would be targeted by this kind of spiritual warfare. I don't think "bad karma" is entirely the problem, but many a New Ager will quickly cast blame on the victim, implying that their difficulties arise because their intentions are not positive enough. I am often amazed at the lack of compassion displayed by many New Age proponents when confronted by another's misfortunes, saying in effect, "Well you create your own reality." True insight, healing and empowerment cannot take place in the face of blame, nor without compassion. Arrogance is not the answer and having a beginner's mind, as the Buddhists contend, is the first step to become free from suffering.

*Emotional Processing*

In order to avoid attracting and feeding the paranormal virus as it attempts to infect the living cells of our love relationship, we must start with emotional clearing. Pent up emotions and unhealed wounds can cause tension, anger, and depression, and act as a magnetic attractor to more of the same. Once the awareness of unresolved emotions emerges, it is the responsibility of the more aware partner to address these issues. This means learning and practicing reflective, compassionate, verbal communication. I specify verbal because many people may opt for body language or nonverbal communication such as slamming doors, looking away, indirect innuendos, guilt inflictors, passive aggressive antics, or the silent treatment. Smiles and hugs, cuddling, etc., are fine as long as they are genuine. We live in a culture where when we are hurt or angry, the tendency is to communicate indirectly, sometimes hurtfully with punishing behaviors, judgmental criticisms, or violence, which of course is unacceptable. There may come a point in the relationship where one person must be firm in setting boundaries, if the other partner is unwilling to relate in a healthy, communicative, ethical manner.

Emotions are not to be viewed as bad or wrong, they simply are. Often we get stuck in a loop of negative emotions, and can't seem to get it out of our system. This is when counseling, compassionate communication and body-mind exercises can be practiced, with good results. I suggest a counselor who can be objective, empathic, and knowledgeable about the situation, as doing it alone almost never works. I have found that it is better to seek out professional educators, counselors and healers, although support groups are great too.

*Emotional Vampires*

When dealing with a partner who is emotionally "draining" to you, or if you feel he or she is an emotional vampire, then you must take solid, consistent measures to establish healthy boundaries with them. You must know how to set boundaries, or break it off with them before you get hurt – because you will if you stay with such persons. This can be extremely difficult and there are entire books about emotional vampires, narcissists and toxic relationship issues in the suggested reading resources at the end of this book. In cases like Francine and Burt, Michelle and Bernie, Wiz and Koral, Stan and Kundra, Nathan and Jezebel, Gwen and Count Rockula and most of the others, there was evidence of emotional vampirism, psychopathy or outright possession by something really dark, sick and controlling.

Now, I'm not in the business of the wishful thinking that sociopaths and demonically possessed people are worth my time in re-educating or offering healing and support. For the most part, they are dangerous individuals who exhibit despicable behaviors and are best avoided. I am not talking about simple "attached entity" issues or blocked emotional energies. In the case of an attached entity, it is only observed some of the time and is more of an overshadowing or partial possession. I am talking about pathological paranormal features.

For example, a person who is literally taken over by some kind of non-

> **When dealing with a partner who is emotionally "draining" to you, or if you feel he or she is an emotional vampire, then you must take solid, consistent measures to establish healthy boundaries with them.**

human malevolent, parasitic entity, and who exhibits paranormal abilities to vampirize human life force energy. By the time paranormal pathologicals get this bad, they are usually too unaware or unwilling to change or learn more humane ways of relating. If they do get therapy, the progress is slow, and staying with them and being a doormat only encourages abusers and emotional vampires to think their behavior is acceptable. Enabling this behavior is almost as bad as the abuse itself. If you are dealing with an abuser, it is imperative to get professional counseling or even legal protection. In cases of physical violence and manipulative controllers, then honest communication is sometimes best delayed, until you have escaped from their grasp, forever.

I hate to sound negative here but staying in airy-fairy land, thinking all people can be saved or healed from their maladies, is simply unrealistic and may even be dangerous. Sociopaths and narcissists – not to mention demonically oppressed individuals – are usually not amenable to negotiation and fair play, nor to true therapy. By nature they do not, and will not, play fair in love relationships or in divorce proceedings for that matter.

There are professional organizations and therapists who educate and provide counseling for victims of psychopaths, such as Sandra L Brown, M.A. She is the CEO of The Institute for Relational Harm Reduction & Public Pathology Education as well as a psychopathologist, program development specialist, lecturer, and an award-winning author.* Her books include *Counseling Victims of Violence: A Handbook for Helping Professionals, How to Spot a Dangerous Man Before You Get Involved Book and Workbook,* and *Women Who Love Psychopaths.* For those who have the unfortunate karma to be in a relationship with a narcissist, there is an excellent book by Wendy T. Behary, LCSW, called *Disarming the Narcissist: Surviving and Thriving with the Self-Absorbed.* My heart goes out to those afflicted with such ill-fated relationships.

There are other professionals such as Scott Peck, author of the best-selling book, *People of the Lie,* who address the real issue of the hope of healing human evil. Lillian Glass, PhD. is another dedicated counseling professional who wrote the best-seller, *Toxic People.*

*Psychic Vampirism*

A psychic vampire, according to author Michele Belanger of *The Psychic Vampire Codex,* (Weiser Books, 2004) is a person who preys upon the life energies of others. They are not undead as many presume, but living people whose need for vital energy is higher than normal. They live with an insatiable type of hunger which cannot be quenched via food, but only through direct assimilation of life force energies. Psychic vampires can be unconscious feeders of life energies, or they may be aware of feeding. Those who are conscious of their energy needs and true nature are referred to as awakened vampires. However, most persons who are reported to be emotional vampires are likely to be feeding on others unconsciously. They may have simple unresolved emotional traumas, where the repression of core feelings and needs block their own

---

* Sandra L. Brown, Public Psychopathy Education, http://saferelationshipsmagazine.com/about/what-we-believe

Chapter 14: Paranormal Intervention Strategies

psychic energy and forces them to draw it from others.

Emotional vampires tend to be emotionally needy, and are attracted to drama and attention-getting behaviors. These people may have an addictive need to talk for long periods of time about personal problems, remaining in the victim state of circular thinking patterns, where no real resolution of the issue occurs. They feel better after talking your ear off for hours, but afterwards you are left feeling drained.

Vampire, from Wiki Commons

They continue to have the same issues in their lives that never seem to heal or change. This behavior should not be confused with everyday venting about a hard day's work or when someone simply needs to talk about a pressing concern. People with personality disorders such as Borderline, Narcissistic and Histrionic Personality Disorder can fall into an emotional vampire behavior pattern, but they may not be the true psychic vampires that feed consciously.

Psychic vampires, by comparison, are a more lethal form of emotional vampire. They also may be emotionally needy, melodramatic, and attention-getting. But they also have a greater ability to suck energy out of you. They may harbor an attached entity which compels their vampiric energy hunger. Their auras can sometimes can be seen by clairvoyants as different than normal, and may contain long energy tendrils that reach out and feed off the energy of others. In most psychic vampire literature that I have read, there is little or no mention of psychic vampires being possessed or overshadowed by other entities.

In general the psychic vampire – in my opinion – is more likely to have an entity attachment, whereas the emotional vampire may not. It takes a clairvoyant person to be able to detect such an attachment, although Kirlian photography can detect changes in the auric energy field of a person before and after being psychically vampirized. In Joe H. Slate's book, *Psychic Vampires,* he shows many Kirlian photographs of a normal aura, one of a psychic vampire, and those of normal people who have just been psychically fed upon by a psychic vampire. These photographs reveal significant and undeniable changes to the energy fields.*

Unawakened psychic vampires, according to J. M. Dixon's, *Weiser Field Guide to Vampires* may be drama addicts. As Dixon puts it, "a vampire feeding unconsciously may unintentionally seek out high-energy situations, drama filled relationships and even dangerously energetic crowds – all just to temporarily raise her energy to a more comfortable level."**

In my case histories, where the person was conscious of astrally connecting to a partner with paranormal features and energy drains, I believe these individuals were consciously feeding vampires. Some persons who are overshadowed by reptilian entities do know of their condition and capabilities. I believe this to be true in the case of Michelle and Bernie the Reverend. He knew he was "not human" and often referred to himself as Master in private conversations with Michelle,

---

\* An interesting video on this is "Psychic Vampires" at http://www.youtube.com/watch?v=Sz9cEjNFOvs

\*\* J. M. Dixon, *Weiser Field Guide to Vampires* (Weiser Books, 2009), p. 65.

whom he regarded as his "slave."

Astrally visiting a person to feed off of their subtle energies is also known as a type of psychic dream walking. This occurs when a person uses a pre-existing psychic bond to connect with the sleeping mind of another. Dream walking isn't necessarily astral sexual communion, but it can include this energy transfer via a psychic link already established with the partner. If links are already established, they can be easily re-linked via any type of emotion or by simply thinking of the partner. Dream walk visits are usually much more vivid than normal dreams. In fact, some of what was described in Anna and Kaleb's story about telesthesia may actually be a type of astral dream walking in which sexual activity is involved, with sensations that are tangible to one or both partners. In their case, neither one was a psychic vampire, but they did believe their love connection to be orchestrated by alien beings.

The subtle energy sensations that some people can sense, especially in telesthesia, may be due to metaphysical energy structures called tendrils. Psychic vampires, according to J. M. Dixon, have unique subtle energy structures which emanate out of their spirit body. These feeding tendrils are like writhing masses of the same electromagnetic energy that spirits are made of, and they are on the outermost layers of their subtle energy bodies. These tendrils allow the vampire to feed on vital energies from a distance when they are unable to do so by direct contact with a human being. The links between vampire and prey are initiated by locking on similar frequencies, such as things or emotions in common between the two people. Sexual chemistry and sexual intercourse itself is also a preferred method of creating a powerful link for psychic feeding. This should not be confused with true tantric lovemaking, unless of course your lover really is a psychic vampire!

One of the hallmarks of deep psychic feeding is a powerful bond between partners, which is exactly what we see in the Dark Side of Cupid and in my first book, *The Love Bite*. This psychic bond doesn't necessarily need physical, sexual contact to be created or maintained, either. A psychic vampire can simply connect with you on similar frequencies, lock on, then astrally visit for a subtle body sexual "feeding." This is what is commonly reported in my cases, often beginning before a couple gets together and sometimes continuing to occur long after the sexual relationship ended. While some individuals continued to have the astral sex dreams of their former "love bite partners," these may not have been regular dreams but a form of psychic dream walking. Once the link is created, it tends to stay for a long time, especially if the link involved true psychic feeding where an energy transfer or exchange took place. A strong bond between lovers doesn't necessarily indicate psychic feeding, but psychic feeding on deeper energetic levels can only occur in the presence of strong psychic bonds for extended periods of time.

Author and self-proclaimed psychic vampire J. M. Dixon warns potential sexual partners of vampires because "when vampires participate in intercourse, they fully engage every part of their spirit, pushing their feeding tendrils deep into the core of their partners from every angle. It can be an extraordinarily violating experience for the donor, one that few are prepared for."*

He also warns of the dangers inherent of continued deep "feeding" with a psychic vampire. Dixon continues:

"The average vampire becomes dangerous to his donor only after repeated, deeply intimate intercourse feeding sessions. This form of feeding, when done correctly, drains so much energy from the donor that it will take days for her to recover from a single session."

The donor in this passage refers to a willing person who understands the true vampiric nature of his or her sexual partner. The author says this about deep communion:

---

* J. M. Dixon, *Weiser Field Guide to Vampires*, p. 75.

*Chapter 14: Paranormal Intervention Strategies*

"A direct feeding from the core energies of the donor occurs when a vampire pushes his feeding tendrils all the way into one or more of a donor's chakras. This process is said to create a deep and permanent psychic link between the two partners. For days afterward, the vampire should be able to hear his partners thoughts at any given time, often when he doesn't even want to."

The telepathy and empathy have been described by many of my "love bite" experiencers, simply because the connection between their lover was so strong. However, I am not certain either partner in all of the Dark Side of Cupid cases were psychic vampires. But the more narcissistic ones may truly be.

What could be happening with the Dark Side of Cupid is an indirect form of psychic feeding. One partner tends to have the greater psychic vampire features, but instead of being a direct, consciously feeding vampire, the partner is used as a sort of portal for an interdimensional, parasitic entity. The Dark Cupid is accessing the two lovers' energy through some kind of mediated energy transfer. The question may then be, "Is Cupid, or whomever is behind this mask, a psychic vampire?"

One of the disconcerting issues that Dixon brought up with deep psychic feeding or communion with a vampire is the permanent psychic link that will be maintained with the donor or unwitting partner. This powerful connection is often felt as true love for the one being fed upon. For the vampire, the partner may be nothing more than an energy fix or addiction. This may result in unrequited love for the unfortunate ones caught in the nest of psychic feeders, as unintentional as it may be. A hazardous by-product of psychic vampire sexual feeding, is a powerful connection which feels like one's true love or soul mate. Hence, the counterfeit soul-mate connection.

Those persons in my cases who exhibited the more psychopathic and narcissistic features surrounded by paranormal anomalies are, in high probability, psychic vampires. If you find yourself becoming drained around these types of lovers, as shared in the cases of Gwen and Count Rockula and of Michelle and Bernie, you may be in the grips of a psychic vampire. Psychic vampirism can occur, in my opinion, through a partner who is being used somehow as a conduit of energy transference to the "third party entity" as discussed previously in this book. We can only guess who these "third party entities" really are.

## Setting Boundaries with Emotional Vampires

Boundaries are physical, sexual, relational, emotional, and even spiritual. A boundary is a limit or edge that defines you as separate from others, a limit that promotes integrity. We can notice this, when for example a person stands next to you, and there is an invisible space between you and them, which you define as safe and comfortable. A lover can stand closer to you than a friend or business associate. Different relationships have different boundaries.

Emotional boundaries are less visible, but very real. On one extreme, enmeshment happens when a person's feelings are ignored or overpowered by a controlling parent or partner. When one is raised in an abusive environment marked by alcoholism, incest, or other problems, they grow up with poor, diffuse boundaries and have difficulty protecting or defending themselves in the face of danger. This is the blank spot or black hole I mentioned earlier, and which causes someone's internal red flag warning systems to fail when in the presence of danger.

Neglect and lack of emotional or physical closeness between a parent or partner causes one to feel alone, separate, and disconnected. Lack of touching and cuddling early on in one's infancy and childhood can cause a person to be emotionally disconnected later in life. If your emotional and relational boundaries are breached, you also become vulnerable to harm, just as your skin is vulnerable to infection if it becomes scratched. When these invisible boundaries are trespassed by the thoughtless and intrusive actions of others, this is a boundary violation.

Our emotional boundaries define who we are. When boundaries are violated, it is a threat to the self. One way to strengthen our boundaries is to be able to say no. It also means the freedom to say yes, acceptance of our differences, respect for feelings, permission for healthy self-expression, support for our healing process, and respect for our individuality.

> **The consequences of telling the truth about one's experience – especially those of alien abduction – are often met with ridicule and mockery. This compounds the harm done to individuals who have already undergone serious trauma.**

Harm to our boundaries comes from being belittled, mocked, and ridiculed. It also comes from being treated with contempt, sarcasm, shaming, malice, stifling communication, the need to overpower, judgmentalism, abandonment, threats, insecurity, and of course any form of violence and abuse.

One thing I'd like to point out is that in anomalous trauma, the consequences of telling the truth about one's experience – especially those of alien abduction – are often met with ridicule and mockery. This compounds the harm done to individuals who have already undergone serious trauma. We must be free to speak our truths and not hide behind facades just to be accepted in a society where truth-telling is often punished, forcing countless thousands into secrecy. I know because I've had to live it for years, and now counsel others who have had to endure lives of secrecy, leading double lives in an unforgiving world.

Learning how to set boundaries is essential in healthy relationships, and is often done unconsciously in people who've been raised to respect others' boundaries. But when you are dealing with an emotional vampire, you must step it up a notch. Now, there are some folks who are emotionally needy or seem to demand extra attention all the time. But they are not necessarily psychopaths, nor should they be pigeonholed as such. Have you ever had a friend, or co-worker who seemed friendly in the beginning, but later you found them annoying, draining, and time consuming? Perhaps they call you up, or visit just to say hello, but really they just want to emotionally dump on you, unloading all their personal dramas, but rarely give you the same time and energy? Or for what they offer you, a few words in edgewise, the payment of emotional energy is extracted and you feel like more was taken from you than given? This is what it feels like to be relating to an emotional vampire.

Let's take a look at the story of Francine and Burt. Francine felt hurt and used by Burt because of his obvious and insensitive public display online about being in love with another woman, even after they shared intimacy. She also told me that Burt had flocks of women interested in him, and seemed to feed off of the attention of his online "harem." She told me she felt taken advantage of when Burt insisted on receiving a massage in the master bedroom, even though Francine could have refused and had him sleep in the extra bedroom. Burt's sly insistence on a massage – which Francine didn't even remember offering – proceeded into sex much too early in their relationship. But, having poor boundaries, she allowed herself to be taken in by his manipulations. Then, to top off an awkward first date, Francine was visited by a demonic entity which invaded her spiritual space. Even though these red flag behaviors were there, they were overridden by the fact that Francine felt a strong psychic connection and attraction to Burt.

## Chapter 14: Paranormal Intervention Strategies

By Francine's second date, she again felt pressured by Burt's decision to visit on short notice, which basically repeated much of the same behavior from Burt. Francine's efforts to share her feelings with Burt about having sex too soon and his insensitive public comments were met later with indirect jibes and barbs on his public networking site, along with more attacks by the invisible entity, resulting in a draining, emotional ping pong game. It was as if Burt wanted to fish for emotional drama and feed from her like a psychic vampire. Burt got more out of Francine than she got out of him.

We have two issues here: poor boundaries for Francine, and a psychic vampire situation that is likely to be connected to the demonic entity attacks that Francine experienced. Burt isn't simply an emotional vampire, but something much more sinister, even if it is unconscious on his part. How might have Francine dealt with this situation differently, asserting her boundaries?

First off, Francine should have suggested she meet Burt for the first time in a public place. But since that was not convenient because of her earlier offer for him to stay in her extra bedroom, she let it slide. The second scene with Burt asking for a massage because he insisted Francine said she would do so for him in an earlier online communication was clearly a manipulative ploy on Burt's end. Instead of stating clearly that she did not recall making such an offer, and saying "no, not tonight," Francine tried to divert his request by saying the massage table was locked away in the storage closet and hard to get to. This diversion was not enough for Burt, who then said he'd just lie on the bed and she could give him a massage there. This was where Francine felt she didn't really have a right to say no, so she acquiesced.

At this juncture Francine could have said, "Burt, I'm not really comfortable giving you a massage tonight, and to be honest, I don't remember offering one to you. How about you sleep in the other bedroom tonight? Then tomorrow we can take some time to talk, connect, and then maybe see how we feel giving each other a massage?"

If Francine had firmly asserted her boundaries, she may not have been as easily taken in by Burt's persuasiveness. It is also true, that if Burt wasn't the manipulative psychic vampire that he was, it may have been easier for her to assert boundaries. If Burt wasn't such a manipulator, her boundaries may have been respected, even unconsciously, without the clear statement proposed for Francine's "boundary intervention strategy" in the last paragraph. But given the reality of what Burt is, this didn't happen. This boundary-asserting communication effort alone may not have stopped the other problem with the demonic entity and the emotional ping-pong game that ensued later. And that is why a more aggressive intervention strategy must be taken with emotional and psychic vampires.

In the case of Michelle and Bernie the Reverend, the need for emotional and spiritual boundary setting was apparent. Like Francine, Michelle had sex sooner than was characteristic for her. Bernie exhibited unusual hypnotic control over Michelle, especially during sex, violating her boundaries even when she told him not to do things that hurt her, leaving her with bruises. When Michelle noticed the invisible entity attacks and their psychic connection to him, she confronted Bernie with this, but he denied it. Here, Michelle took steps to communicate, confront and exert her boundaries, but she was overpowered by the Reverend's paranormal hypnotic control over her. Even after Michelle confronted Bernie about the entity working through him, he openly showed her how he could easily control her mentally and physically with seemingly no effort, using mockery.

What we are seeing here is a psychopathic display of control and utter disrespect for Michelle, regardless of her ability to communicate and assert her boundaries. On other topics Michelle could communicate to Bernie, but when it came to sex and religious issues, it was quite a different situation. He also displayed jealousy and judgmental condemnation in regards to her divorced status, assaulting her self-worth. Michelle did break off the relationship with Bernie, but the vicious, controlling, interdimensional lizard entity would not leave her alone. It invaded her psychic space, affecting her physical energy levels and causing undue emotional turmoil.

I had to wonder what Jesus Christ really meant when he said some people are like wolves in sheep's clothing. I've counseled at least five cases where a dark energy vampire influenced a religious guru type of figure that astrally attacked the victim. I'd just like to point out that Michelle and Bernie's love bite is not an isolated case of such reports. Most are too hurt, confused or scared to talk about it.

I'd like to point out too, when we are dealing with psychic vampires of the psychopathic paranormal type, regular communication skills and asserting boundaries are often completely ignored and overpowered by the psychopath's desires. Here we need a stronger paranormal intervention strategy. In Michelle's case she sought out a shaman, did cleansing ceremonies with group prayer, and smudged her personal space with sage regularly. This is a Native American tradition to clear one's space of dark spirits or congested energies. In addition to this, I assisted her in counseling, support, and hypnotic neurolinguistic methods to reconnect with her inner soul power, deleting alien energy attachments and parasitic beings. Michelle prayed daily and repeated affirmations to connect with her soul power to deflect the attached entity, break off psychic links and empower herself.

*Spiritual Empowerment*

Even if we have been dedicated in our spiritual faith with prayer and other forms of spiritual practice, we can still get parasitic and energy attachments – like those discussed in the aforementioned case histories. Depending on one's faith, there are a number of strategies to choose from:

*Prayer requesting a higher power to assist you*
- Praying for others before ourselves
- Praying alone or in groups

*Spiritual release work, that involves entity detachments and energy clearings*
- Hypnotherapy and neurolinguistic programming to tap into the power of the subconscious mind and soul to assist in clearing. Dr. Corrado Malanga's Flash Mental Simulation. (SIMBAD and FMS)[*]
- Deliverance, exorcisms
- Shamanic soul retrievals and spirit-entity releases
- The 7-Day Psychic Protection Plan by Joe H. Slate.[**]
- Chapter 9 of Robert Bruce's book, *The Practical Psychic Self-Defense Handbook: A Survival Guide.*[***]
- Daily meditation and visualizations that actively clear out energies or parasites that are not yours, with a therapist, clergy, healer or alone.

*Service to Others*
- Supporting others in their healing and growth journey
- Practicing kindness and compassion
- Generosity
- Offering personal service or resources to those less able; volunteer work
- Dedicating your service and spiritual practice for the

---

[*] Malanga, Corrado, Ph. D., http://flashmentalsimulation.wordpress.com/corradomalanga/

[**] Slate, Joe, Ph.D., *Psychic Empowerment: A 7-Day Plan for Self-Development*, (Llewellyn's Strategies for Success, 1997

[***] Bruce, Robert, *The Practical Psychic Self-Defense Handbook: A Survival Guide*, (Hampton Roads, 2011)

benefit of others to free those still enslaved and in suffering (The Buddhist Bodhisattva ideal)
- Gratitude, gratitude, gratitude
- Community singing, dancing and sacred ceremony dedicated to healing

One of the things I admire about Buddhist philosophy is the way in which Buddhists view and realize the value of spiritual power to overcome obstacles to enlightenment. Other faiths may hold this to be true, too. It is the cultivation of virtue. The greater the virtue, the greater one's spiritual power. Virtue is attained through offering selfless service from the heart to help free others from suffering and the causes of suffering. It can also be understood as the Bodhisattva ideal. When we can rise above purely self-serving motivations is when, I believe, the divine power kicks in to assist us.

In Sanskrit terminology a bhakti yoga practice is all about devotional love practices, living from the heart. It may include all of the above and more.

Cultivation of joy is a great way to clear out negative emotions or spiritual energies. Things that can bring a person joy are:
- Walking along the beach
- Watching sunrise and sunset
- Nature hikes
- Devotional singing, gospel spiritual songs, opera
- Drumming & singing and dancing ceremonies
- Group prayer
- Dancing with a partner
- Heart centered yoga such as Hatha yoga
- Rejoicing in the good deeds of others
- Meditation on gratitude
- Good humor, laughter

A proactive strategy is to build the community you value. If we want to have more compassionate communication and emotional support in our lives, we must build it. If we want more powerful spiritual fellowship, we must reprioritize our time and attention so that spiritual values and practices are number one. In my life, compassionate communication is a spiritual practice. It has to start from the core of our heart and expand outwards in our relationships via concrete communication skills. It must be learned.

Living from the heart authentically gives us the spiritual power to overcome suffering. In the next chapter I will address the grieving and bereavement process.

# Chapter 15

# Grieving the Loss of Your Lover

Grieving from the loss of a lover is an important part of the healing journey. The length of healing indicated the depth of pain that so many carried for years. I believe that the pain of a Dark Side of Cupid relationship is much more traumatic and emotionally devastating than most love relationship break ups. In general, the more intense the love connection was, the greater the pain. The length of healing for seventeen respondents to my study are shown in the table below.

| Time to Heal | Number | Percentage % |
|---|---|---|
| 0-2 years | 5/17 | 29 |
| 2-5 years | 4/17 | 24 |
| 5-16 years | 6/17 | 35 |
| still married | 2/17 | 12 |

Thirty-five percent of the people in my study took from five to sixteen years to heal. This is a long time, considering that most of these love affairs lasted for less time than was spent healing and grieving the loss. Kundra spent 16 years healing, and still suffers health issues that started when in relationship with Stan. Gwen, even though she is only two years past the break up from her emotional vampire lover, is barely out of the shock and denial phase and only starting her grieving process. Amy, whose love affair with the doctor lasted ten years, is still in the grieving process and vacillates between the various stages of grief. Others such as Francine, Nathan, and Michelle, had complicated grieving issues related to former toxic relationships.

*Grief*

The grief of a loss, whether it is the death of a loved one, a relationship breakup, or a divorce, goes through several stages. These stages are a spontaneous chain of events and feelings that start with: 1) shock and denial, 2) anger, 3) depression, 4) bargaining and magic, 5) resolution and acceptance. These stages do not necessarily follow in the exact order shown, and may vacillate between phases.

Mourning the loss of a lover can take weeks, months, or years, depending on the person and their unique situation. Some people may stay in the shock and denial stage for a long time, especially if there is an addiction going on to numb their pain. Anger is a difficult issue, and many can stay in the anger and blame phase forever. During the magical and bargaining phase, the person may make silent bargains with God, such as, "If only I do such and such, then the pain will go away." In an effort to skip past the grief, one might engage in ritualistic behavior such as compulsive hand washing or vowing never to date such a person again, to avoid the same mistake made with the past lover. A person who feels rejected by an unfaithful partner may go in endless circles of trying to determine what they did wrong that caused the other person to hurt them. Even if the individual had no control over their partner's behavior, they may still feel that they can gain control through such actions.

Depression and sadness can go together, although true clinical depression is different from sadness. Sadness is an appropriate response to upsetting events, and can usually be relieved by an emotional outlet such as crying. Depression is a longer lasting effect of repression and turning inward of unresolved anger, though it can also be caused by a biochemical imbalance. In the grieving process, sadness will pass with time, but depression may remain. The mourning process can take days, weeks, months, or years, and may also be intermittent. Sporadic episodes can be sparked by significant dates, anniversaries, or places you liked to go with your lover.

The final stages of mourning, those of resolution and acceptance, involve forgiveness. This can take some time, especially if the relationship involved a psychopath whose behaviors were extremely damaging and malicious. Compounded by paranormal anomalies and psychic-emotional vampirism – as happens on the more lethal end of the spectrum of the Dark Side of Cupid – the healing process can take quite a long time. I believe this involvement of paranormal factors is the reason why more than one-third of my cases needed such a long time to heal.

## Factors in Grieving

Grief and mourning do not decline in a steady, linear fashion. They fluctuate over time and are affected by many variables. Grieving is a process, involving many transitions and changes. Priorities and concerns may change. It may be necessary to slow down, to take time for self-reflection, and to break off unsupportive associations. The impact of grief can hit you like a ton of bricks. You may realize that you need a lot of solitude and that old friends no longer serve your new priorities and needs. This can be an additional stress, as in cases of divorce, where not only is the relationship ended and the home gone, but many friends lost as well. During this transitional period, it is especially important to create a support network of friends who share your views on the importance of healing, recovery, and growth.

Until the mourning process is complete, new life situations can trigger old memories and past grief. This is natural. Ignoring grief doesn't make it go away, as much as we may wish it would. Allow yourself to experience the emotions rather than suppressing them, and share your feelings honestly with caring friends, relatives, or counselors who will listen without judging and who will allow you to work through your emotions rather than try to move you out of them. Responses such as, "keep your chin up," "carry on," or "just don't worry, be happy" are not helpful, no matter how well intended they may be.

Post-traumatic stress is common following an encounter with the Dark Side of Cupid, because one is dealing not only with the loss of a partner, but also with reality-shattering challenges to one's core beliefs. Sometimes grief must be suppressed in order to cope with the ongoing demands of daily living and survival. Numbness serves a valuable purpose at the beginning of a breakup because it helps soften the blow, and you are more able to tolerate the unpleasant truth. For example, the realization that your partner was a full-blown, psychopathic, psychic vampire with malevolent intentions toward you is a horribly painful shock. Especially if you were in a long-term relationship with someone who lived a double life, such a realization can be extremely traumatic. A period of numbness can allow your mind to grow accustomed to the facts without overwhelming you with emotion.

Times like these are great opportunities to embrace your spirituality. In Anna's story, her spiritual path in shamanism led her to a greater ability to cope, and allowed her the space she needed to realize deeper insights that might not have occurred had she not embraced her healing journey. We have the freedom to embrace our spirituality and our own unique ways of making it sacred by creating personal ritual to give closure to devastating, emotional losses.

Often we become angry with God because of the death of a soul mate relationship. A powerful, deep soul connection that we believed would last forever and had great significance to us, with all its attendant signs and portents, came to an ugly end. Being angry with God for such losses is a normal part of the grieving process. But remember, having strong personal faith does not protect you from needing to talk about your thoughts, new beliefs, and feelings. Expressing faith is good, but not as a way to avoid doing the healing and recovery work that real grieving demands. Religion can be healing and supportive, offering a gift of grace, or it can be abused as an addiction and an excuse to avoid reality. Remember that "God helps those who help themselves."

Grief can be resurrected after periods of calm and acceptance when catalyzed by events like birthdays, holidays, hearing a song from that time period, or going to a favorite restaurant. These periods are not unhealthy in themselves. Feelings will arise whether you try to repress them or not, so allow yourself to experience the feelings and then let them go. Sometimes they are simple reminders that we need more time and space to heal, because if this is not heeded, one can end up in a disastrous rebound relationship.

Incomplete grief is insidious because so often we do not realize what pain we hold until we are faced with new relationships. We may find that we are resistant to forming new relationships, dating, or other major life changes because of unresolved grief and massive trust issues. These resistant patterns of change can bring with them feelings of guilt, shame, and anger at oneself and others for not being strong enough to "get over it." And, as so often happens in cases of divorce, where a Dark Side of Cupid match happened to be a rebound love affair – the pain is twice as strong because the new loss brings up the unresolved aspects of the old one that have yet to be grieved.

The timing and duration of the grief will be determined by:
- Your own commitment to heal
- Your intention to let go of the lover, as wonderful as the connection was
- Your willingness to experience the pain in order to let it go
- Your state of health and energy
- Your willingness to express feelings in multiple ways
- The quality of support available to you

- Your courage to get out of yourself and begin to explore and experiment with what brings value and quality of life back to you

*Self-Forgiveness*

It is necessary to forgive oneself for getting involved in a Dark Side of Cupid relationship before we can even try to forgive another person, let alone heal. Self-forgiveness requires a level of inner empathy, and a willingness to face our own

> **It is necessary to forgive oneself for getting involved in a Dark Side of Cupid relationship before we can even try to forgive another person, let alone heal.**

feelings squarely when they do arise. When grief hasn't fully resolved itself, we can stay angry with ourselves for being stupid enough to get involved with the one who hurt us. Or we can stay angry with the other person, or blame Cupid for the pain we endured. Either way, healing cannot take place until we are willing to work through whatever feelings we are experiencing. Finding the courage to face deep emotional pain is the first step to rising out of it, as paradoxical as it sounds. The truth is, the pain doesn't last forever, but when we feel it, it seems like it will be with us for the rest of our life.

*When Grief Doesn't Heal*

Normally, the grieving process may include periods of depression, anger, withdrawal and apathy. It's natural for a grieving person to feel he or she will never be happy or in a love relationship again. In time, these feelings will become fewer and more sporadic, and will become interspersed with a gradual return of energy and a reinvestment in life.

But sometimes grief doesn't lessen over time. There are many reasons why the healing process may be delayed. In the Dark Side of Cupid, one must recognize that a major shift in perception, beliefs, and worldview may have taken place on top of the loss of a lover with whom we felt an incredible connection. The paranormal anomalies in conjunction with any form of emotional vampirism can shatter one's feelings of safety, and if your partner was a psychopath or narcissist overshadowed by a non-human entity, we have a lot of issues to deal with, to put it mildly! In fact, most of my cases that took greater than five years to heal were afflicted with post traumatic stress disorder (PTSD).

The main reasons why grief becomes complicated can be:
1. Lack of self-trust, feeling unable to endure the pain
2. Lack of support with someone who offers a safe environment in which to grieve or tell your story (Again, a reminder why I am writing this book!)
3. Experience of multiple losses, or emotional overload due to too many losses in a short period of time
4. Loss of meaning, when all meaning was invested in the lover, lacking purpose to continue
5. Previous unresolved losses, especially childhood and relationship abuse
6. Excessive or prolonged use of drugs and/or alcohol
7. Traumatic or unanticipated loss where there is no opportunity to develop coping strategies
8. Poor health, mental or physical, lack of energy or stamina to handle the grief
9. Horrendous loss due to malice, evil, violence, and the profound violation of personal safety and survival needs where psychic numbing contributes to delayed or inhibited grief.
10. Unresolved or conflicted feelings toward the lover whom you left or who left you

11. Pre-existing pathology or dysfunction, i.e., chronic severe depression, or PTSD

The big hitters on this list with the Dark Side of Cupid are 2, 10, and 11. Lack of support, unresolved feelings toward the lost lover, and pre-existing pathologies go hand in hand because when something happens outside of the normal range of human experience, it becomes harder to believe and therefore harder to cope with. This compounds the difficulty of healing, since it is difficult to find supportive people who have the ability to think outside the box, and who also have the empathy to help face your feelings, not to mention their own. In 10, the unresolved, ambivalent feelings occur when a powerful connection still lingers. The yearning for the lover in either partner seems to maintain an inexplicable psychic connection that makes healing and moving on much more difficult.

The second most common factors are 3 and 5. Factor 3 concerns previous multiple losses without adequate time to cope, while factor 5 is about childhood abuse and/or former relationship abuse. These are potent vulnerability factors, but even persons such as Nathan and Anna, who did not have former abuse issues, still got hit by the Dark Side of Cupid with traumatic consequences. What differed with them is that their relationship did not last as long, and was therefore not as devastating as those with longer-term dysfunctional relationships.

*Forgiveness*

There is something paradoxical about forgiveness. When you have been wronged by another, it's logical to think that that person does not deserve forgiveness. It's one thing to understand that someone did not intend to harm you, and to forgive their lack of awareness. But in cases of psychopaths with malicious and deceitful intent, it is like being the victim of a crime, not a simple lovers' quarrel.

Forgiveness requires that we step beyond the rational mind, and into the chambers of the soul. You must set aside your reasoning mind and work from the heart. This is the part of the healing process that requires us to reach out to God and into the depth of our own emotions. We must want to forgive, but we often do not really understand what forgiveness is. It is not a one-time event, but a process, just as grieving is a process.

Forgiveness does not necessarily require reconciliation. It can be demonstrated by giving a gift that the other may accept or reject, or might not even know about. It can be in the heart

> **Forgiveness requires that we step beyond the rational mind, and into the chambers of the soul. You must set aside your reasoning mind and work from the heart.**

of the forgiver. Reconciliation requires forgiveness in order for the relationship to be restored.

Forgiveness does not mean condoning harmful behavior, just dealing with it.

Forgiveness does not mean trusting the one who harmed you.

Forgiveness is not forgetting, for deep hurts usually cannot be wiped out of one's memory.

Forgiveness is dealing with another person's offense in a way that helps the forgiver find healing and move forward with their life.

Forgiveness is giving up resentment and vengeance, and fostering compassion for the inflictor of pain.

When we forgive, we release ourselves from the shackles and the ties that bind us to the one who hurt us.

Forgiveness is a gift of grace when we truly desire to forgive, and allow divine help to enter our hearts.

There are five steps in granting forgiveness:
- Acknowledge the anger and hurt caused by the lost lover and/or offenses.
- Resolve not to inflict, or even to desire, punishment or vengeance towards the offender.
- Be willing to consider the offender's perspective. Try to understand his or her behavior and beliefs.
- Decide to accept the hurt without unloading it on the offender, or on others.
- Extend goodwill and compassion to the offender, even if only in your private thoughts. This releases the offended from the offense.

Of course this process is easier said than done. It takes emotional integrity and spiritual faith in a higher power that has greater wisdom and compassion than your own logical, reasoning mind. Rejection of forgiveness leads to other hurts. Anger, if not kept in check, can lead to sickness, conflicts, or even violence. This is the cyclic anger phase, which is almost like an addiction, because it prevents the rising of deeper emotions of loss and grief to the surface in order to be purged out of one's heart.

Some people who have been deeply hurt do develop a negative addiction or a chronic negative attitude expressed in frequent anger, rejection, and suspicion. In situations where the abuse is continual, healing is very difficult. Lack of forgiveness and persistent anger are two of the surest ways to get stuck in our grief. We cannot fully feel, receive, or give love to others if we are stuck in our hurt and grief. Sadly, many of us remain in this suspended state of disconnection without even realizing it, after we have been deeply hurt.

Healing from an encounter with the Dark Side of Cupid

lies in the willingness to feel our pain, to experience it fully, and to offer up what we cannot handle to God. In essence, God really is our deeper heart, our soul essence that holds timeless wisdom and the gift of divine grace. I don't believe God ever meant for us to deal with such pain alone, without the helpful support of a friend or loved one.

Reconciling your grief does not always happen quickly. Grief, like forgiveness, is a process rather than an event. Be patient and tolerant with yourself. It's not true that you won't ever be happy or find your true love or soul mate, though it may feel that way for a while. It is simply that you will never exactly be the same as you were before.

In closing, I'd like to share a poem my sister, Pamela Jacobs, wrote many years ago after a lost love affair. It is one of my favorites, because she has the gift of being able to tap into the heart of grace through poetry.

*Lost Love*

Love is not lost
to those who understand.
The badge of pain
takes its toll
on all souls forever.
A reminder to what was reality
but is now only wisdom.

Oh, the pain is true!
Eyes do not hide
to what was just
another time.

Oh poor child,
I see your troubled past
and bleed with you.
Never give up caring, trying, fighting.
That little bud
will be a perfect flower someday.

Chapter 16

# Is there a Light Side of Cupid?

The question about whether Cupid has a light side has been repeatedly asked of me, as well as whether aliens can orchestrate happy, harmonious relationships. Based on my own case studies of those who experience alien-orchestrated relationships, the answer is yes.

But they are few. The "happy and harmonious" orchestrated love relationships are in the minority. It appears that Cupid, like aliens, has a good and bad side, and seems to playing both sides of the fence.

I have great interest in hearing about couples that believe divine forces have brought them together, whether they are soul mates or twin souls. Comparing the stories from Arielle Ford's *Hot Chocolate for the Mystical Lover*,[*] I am convinced these were "positive" orchestrated relationships which lasted a number of years, and exhibited neither the high amount of paranormal activity nor the emotional draining that is a hallmark of the Dark Side of Cupid. Many of Arielle Ford's couples reported experiencing precognitive dreams of meeting their future partner, as well as synchronistic events which they believed to be either an answer to prayer, or direct results of efforts in positive manifestation. Empathy and shared interests were common with these individuals, whose focus tended to be on spirituality and personal growth. If they experienced conflict, as most couples eventually do, it was not accompanied by the crashing lows, emotional draining, manipulation, or

---

[*] Ford, Arielle, *Hot Chocolate for the Mystical Lover: 101 True Stories of Soul Mates Brought Together By Divine Intervention*, (Penguin Books, 1999).

extended paranormal activity, which characterize the Dark Side of Cupid.

In their book, *Twin Souls,*[*] Patricia Joudry and Maurie Pressman relate several stories of couples brought together by unusual circumstances. Some of these include experiencing blissful sexual unions astrally or in dreams. Clairvoyance was enhanced for one couple after experiencing astral unions on higher dimensions. Other couples claim they were compelled to do or say something that was out of character for them, which resulted in meeting their soul mate or twin soul.

According to the authors, the difference between a twin soul relationship and a non-soul mate situation, is that "…in a good relationship, two people proceed in harmony, reconciling their conflicting views; but the twin-soul relationship is founded on a fundamental sense of oneness: oneness of vision, oneness of purpose, oneness of feeling. Twin souls do not pull their separate ways, except briefly and temporarily at the personality level. They progress as one, no longer hobbled by difference in pace or direction. This is the reason their advance is so swift once the connection has been made."

In twin soul relationships, both persons are usually on parallel spiritual paths or extended personal growth work that reached a plateau where they were ready to meet their "other half." There was no emotional manipulation or psychic vampirism at all. The connections between twin souls were nearly telepathic in some cases, but in ways that brought great satisfaction, harmony and oneness of spiritual purpose in life. These people were spiritually focused and service-oriented.

The authors also pointed out the reality of evil in the world and forces that act to obstruct true twin soul communion, since it is such a powerful positive force in the world. I have seen this exhibited in a few of my own unpublished cases. It is very

---

[*] Joudry, Patricia and Pressman, Maurie D., M.D. *Twin Souls: Finding Your True Spiritual Partner*, (Hazeldon, 2000).

possible that a conspiracy does indeed exist against the power of true love and real soul mate connections.

I correspond with a few couples who suspect they were put together by alien beings, and whose relationship is beneficial for both parties. One couple in particular cherishes the powerful bond and connection they feel, and they are making the relationship work amidst disruptive paranormal activity. Both partners are exceptionally aware of the supernatural circumstances, and due to that awareness and intention to stay together, it is more positive than the relationships that have been described in this book.

On the whole, the greater the awareness of the couple, and the more they work to protect the strong bond between them, the greater the chance they have to overcome whatever forces that may act to break them apart. This is a great test of true love, whether they are twin souls, soul mates, or not.

I believe the Dark Side of Cupid represents an obstructive force, a.k.a., the paranormal viral factor, which acts to forge a counterfeit soul mate connection. This may either be intended to disrupt the couple's spiritual path, or it may simply be a situation of psychic vampirism. In either case, the human soul may very well be at stake, and it would behoove us to nurture love to its fullest in order to protect our souls from these invasive beings.

Sometimes our only way of truly knowing a real soul-mate love connection is to experience what it is not. We humans learn from our mistakes, and what was a painful experience can be transformed into the wisdom needed to discern true love, and the resilience to deflect all that is not in our best interest.

Now that we know what darkness can descend to obstruct our path, we are more prepared for the expansive joy of the light of love. Just as the roots of a tree must descend into the soil below to strengthen its foundation in the earth, so too will its deeply rooted foundation provide the strength to rise above and grow to its fullest potential in beauty.

*Chapter 16: Is there a Light Side of Cupid?*

*It is wrong to think that Love comes from
long companionship or persevering courtship.
Love is the offspring of a spiritual affinity,
and unless that affinity is created IN A MOMENT,
it will not be created in years or even generations.*
~ Kahlil Gibran ~

# Conclusion

Now that we have learned how to recognize the patterns of supernatural interference in our love relationships, we are more able to trust our instincts when something out of the ordinary comes knocking on our door. Recognizing the unholy triad of the dark side of Cupid, the magical/paranormal, high emotional drama, and energy vampirism, we have no more need to fear these powerful love affairs. With the light of understanding and empathic support we can tread these waters with greater stability and confidence. By enhancing our own awareness of the supernatural in our love relationships, we now have the tools to discern what is right for us.

Self-empowerment is gradually achieved with emotional intelligence and the development of empathy for ourselves first, and then for others. Our willingness and courage to step into our feelings, to experience them fully and to let them go, will lead us to healing and wholeness. Emotional integrity and awareness will protect us from psychic energy predators. There is no need to be buffeted about on an emotional roller coaster, or to be a victim of psychic vampirism or other attack.

Now that we can understand what our own red flag warnings are, we can listen to our inner voice with greater awareness and confidence. When entering a love relationship with a strong psychic connection, we are able to hear that inner voice, to pay attention to our psychic energy levels, and to notice our emotional response. We can now quickly recognize the signs and symptoms of supernatural relationship interference, emotional depletion and psychic vampirism.

When faced with a Dark Side of Cupid love connection, we are now able to call on our knowledge of compassionate communication skills and paranormal intervention strategies, and put them into practice. We can decide whether to engage in that powerful psychic connection with a new lover, or to set firmer boundaries that protect us from the roller coaster of high emotional drama or psychic vampirism. We have the power to choose to continue the love affair, or to let it go.

We can engage in spiritual empowerment practices and discover a life of greater spiritual meaning and psychic protection with a renewed sense of well being. We realize there is no reason to fear the paranormal in our lives or relationships, and that supernatural interferences can occur within neutral or even benevolent ways. Waking up to this reality need not be a shocking or painful experience, but can be embraced with our unique spirituality as a healing journey of greater wisdom and self-empowerment.

Now that we have the insights to discern what a true soul mate connection is, and what it is not, we can decide to nurture what we have with our lover with more patience and compassion, or we can let it go with greater understanding, acceptance, and self-respect. By embracing our healing journey after we have lost a lover, we can build the inner resources to attract and be ready for our true beloved.

Humanity's greatest gift and power is the consummation of true love between soul-connected lovers in a harmonious dance of yearning, ecstatic union, and repose. The joy, power, and bliss generated in a true soul-mate or even twin soul relationship is certainly the greatest mystery we can experience while in our earthly bodies.

There is something about the human soul which is a great enigma even to the beings who seem to be mediating our connection with the divine. It is as if these entities, Cupid in particular, play both sides of the fence. Some seem to envy us, hurling punishments, accusations, and undeserved suffering, jealous of the attention our beauty can bestow upon us. The old myths cater to the beliefs that in order to commune with our divine Beloved, we must first purify ourselves through countless tests and trials, justifying the suffering of intense emotional and spiritual anguish.

The precious gem of our immortal soul seems to be entrapped in our physical bodies. If the soul is truly an inherent aspect of being human, why would we need to fight for it, begging for an external God to grant us immortality? Perhaps true love is the fast track to immortality. I believe true love happens when we meet the Beloved, such as what is described in the Bible as the inner bridal chamber, with the Beloved of our soul. Sufi mystics, for example, also speak of the Beloved and engage in heart devotional spiritual practices. This meeting of the Beloved happens within the chamber of our heart and soul. Once this occurs, one's state of being shifts to a higher vibration, where divine unconditional love flows spontaneously for the benefit of others. It is unselfish. Only then can this be reflected in our outer world for the true lover-beloved relationship.

Divine love comes from a place that is beyond time and space. It is the primordial aspect of our soul. Its essence is immortal because it is pre-existent within our souls. Hence, if this is true, as many mystical traditions and religions such as Buddhism assert, why would we need to pray and beg for this? It already exists within each one of us who has a soul. Perhaps the prayer would more appropriately be for the remembrance of our soul, to reconnect with the Beloved we have always known.

What is it about the Dark Side of Cupid that can so cleverly deceive us into believing we have found true love, only to be led on a wild chase of emotionally draining dramas and paranormal activity? Is this some kind of cosmic spiritual test for those of us who are on a quest for wisdom and true love? Are these beings – who appear to be energy vampires – acting as a sort of mediated presence for an ultimate shamanic initiation in our lives under an even higher level of spiritual authority?

Perhaps we need to contemplate who is trying to get our attention and wake us up. I believe we do have the answers within the depths of our soul. Each individual must discover this for themselves.

# Appendix

These interviews have been added as an addendum to the case involving Maarit and Bjorn, as Maarit is an alien abductee from birth and has experienced military abductions (MILABs). For those not familiar with abduction and MILAB testimonies, I encourage readers to visit my web site at www.evelorgen.com.

*Interview with Maarit, a Scandinavian Milab-ReAB*
*By Eve Lorgen 4/07/011*

Synopsis of Maarit's Interview

*Disclaimer:* This is a witness testimony of a military abductee Re-Ab,(an alien abductee who has had military abductions also) and contains disturbing material and is not recommended reading for those who cannot handle the reality of malevolent alien abductions or shadow government activities. I cannot vow to the absolute facts of all of this testimony, nor all of Maarit's opinions. This is offered as another piece of the puzzle exploring the MILAB issue, and as an extension of the work of the late Dr. Karla Turner and Barbara Bartholic, as well as my own contribution. It is not meant to be fear based, but as a "wake up call" testimony to acknowledge those who should not have to live lives of harassment, oppression and secrecy.

This interview is with a female MILAB-abductee from Scandinavia named Maarit. She chose to use a pseudonym to protect her anonymity. She contacted me in late 2010 to share her testimony of alien abductions and subsequent military abductions following her pregnancy with her son in 2005. I interviewed Maarit because she is one of a handful of very lucid abductees, those who can recall a good portion of their abduction-related experiences without the use of hypnosis.

Although she has neuroimmunological health issues related to multiple sclerosis, I believe her to be mentally intact and credible. She is also highly psychic and can lucid dream – the ability to be conscious and aware during the dream state. This has enabled her to regain greater degrees of awareness during her alien and military abductions. A large component of her military abductions involved being used as a guinea pig with colluding pharmaceutical-medical companies who work in conjunction with the shadow government on MILABs.

Maarit shares her understanding of how and why she is "genetically modified" – a hybrid if you will – and how this figures into her neurophysiologic and immunological issues with multiple sclerosis and an Rh-negative blood type.

Maarit explains how her life and marriage have been completely orchestrated by her handlers, who are primarily Draconian, reptilian, and military. She has observed many species of ETs in her experiences and recalls being in DUMBs (Deep Underground Military Bases). She also recalls being inside a nuclear silo with dark winged, Draconian entities. She discusses her understanding of the genetic and energetic-soul matrix, vibrational aspects of hybrids, and the alien soul recycling technology. She had an experience similar to Ted Rice of Dr. Karla Turner's *Masquerade of Angels*, involving having her consciousness transferred into a "black box" and placed into a cloned body.

Although hybrids are now a focal interest in current abduction research, she asserts the most important aspects we need to focus on is how aliens – specifically reptilians – can manipulate, orchestrate and interfere with our relationships. Maarit awakened to her experiences after more memories surfaced, which triggered the realization of malevolent and mind controlling elements in her abductions. The use of Virtual Reality (VRE) brain entrainment technology is done to control consciousness, and is hooked up once an abductee is implanted. One of her screen memories installed by Draconian entities involved seeing beatific, New Agey, dolphin scenes upon awakening from an abduction experience. Beneath this screen memory was an abduction in an underground base. She admitted to having previously promoted popular "benevolent ET experiences" on a Scandinavian radio talk show before becoming lucid to the reality of the deceptive, mind controlling nature of her abductions. Now, she is fighting back, regaining her lucidity and spiritual resilience. She wants us to know humans can fight back for their awareness and freedom. Awareness is the key to empowerment.

*Tell me a bit about how you discovered you had ET experiences, and your initial beliefs about alien/abduction and contact? What shifted your beliefs about the true nature of ETs and your experiences, any particular incidents which "broke the programming" of what the more popular UFO groups and researchers were promoting?*

Before we start, I would like to thank Eve Lorgen for her work, which bravely goes to the dark side of this alien phenomena. I contacted her while I was frustrated and tired. Her open heart and integrity as a researcher and therapist made a huge impact on me. I consider our intensive correspondence as a major turning point in my life. She offered her presence for a total stranger, not so many willing to do these days. In the UFO-field there are not so many researchers who are willing to step out of the comfort zone of contactee oriented happy UFO-scenarios. Only by realizing the alien manipulative agenda we can achieve autonomy for our consciousnesses as a human race.

First of all, I consider myself to be an abductee – being

unwillingly used by aliens and military for several purposes. Because I have been manipulated, drugged, and mind controlled by humans and aliens, I do not use the term contactee. In my experiences, there is no reciprocal nuance to be observed, as in cases of alleged contactee people. I do not consider myself to be special or chosen in any way. I don't have any channeled information to offer. All I can offer is question after question.

When I refer to term shadow government/people, I mean globally operating companies related to medical warfare operatives as well as factions of military/intelligent groups. Which ones, I don't know for certain.

I can divide my alien encounters in two different parts. One part of this alien encounter began before I was even born. I have conscious memories of that time when I was in another, subtle form of existence and forced unwillingly to manifest in this three-dimensional universe as we humans observe it now. I consider the essence of my spiritual being to be alien, per se. I remember how I was shown different parental alternatives to choose from. The connecting link between these human couples was some sort of DNA structure. My consciousness moved into my infant human body just before labor and I was fully aware of these memories even when I was a baby. After a while the normal neurological adjusting begun and I saw myself as a "normal" child with heightened psychic abilities.

The second part of my "human" experience with alien encounters began in childhood at 4 years old, and I knew I was not alone. When I woke up, there was blood on my pillow and I knew "somebody" stuck something into my nose. I constantly saw scary dreams and woke up in terror. These things happened during the time when I was 4-7 years old. But as funny as it sounds, during the childhood I do not have any clear memories of these beings that were terrorizing me or how they look liked. But when I saw a picture of a UFO, I knew "they" were the ones.

Another wave of consciously remembered encounters happened, as usual, during my teens. Even as a child I was fascinated by astronomy, nuclear physics, philosophical principles related to existence and ontology. I was more and more "humanized" as whole. I wanted to find the solution, the ultimate matrix for meta-consciousness and all that I could find at that time was the New-Age movement and the shallow answers it had to offer.

Even when I was fairly aware of being abducted at that time (16 -30 years old) that these encounters were not benevolent, I was mentally forced to interpret my experiences as such. The New-Age way to look these alien encounters during 80's and 90's was so full of subjective reasoning and pressure. Mostly because here in Scandinavia some the UFO-researchers are highly contactee oriented. And the material these "certain" new age-minded UFO-researchers produced was directly linked to their publishing business.

In Scandinavia we were not given proper options in which we could judge the characters of the alien encounters by ourselves. I was once even on the local radio telling (when I was still into the New Age perspective) about these lovely space brothers, which are here to lift our vibrations, because I did not want to be shut out from the community of friends I was related to during that period of time. At that time I was just one piece of this manipulative machinery, which was planned to misdirect people by giving them highly calculated answers to solve their nocturnal horrifying problems. And I did my job, but not with smiling face.

As I got older, the abductions began to be physically more real. I could remember things which did not suit the concept of contactee based rhetoric. My ovum was harvested on regular basis and I saw constant marks like sudden bruises, straight cuts, triangular rashes, scoop marks, burned like areas in my ankles, needle marks on my forehead and nose with the upper layer of dermis removed on my body after these episodes. I could not lie to myself anymore about the nature of these encounters. They were malevolent, controlling and they affected my consciousness and memories in a suppressive manner. Not once was I given a straight answer by the abductors for the alien agenda.

At that time I found myself being alone. Suddenly after that conscious realization, of questioning the aliens motives as not being "good", was when I was isolated mentally and socially via certain episodes in my life. I was carrying a secret no one publicly would respond to in the UFO-field here in Scandinavia. So I felt I was living a private hell in front of many ignorant eyes.

The shift from New-Age beliefs to more an objective state of mind was subtle but very solid and inevitable concerning my realization of the true nature of these alien abductions. The MILAB involvement however, began when I was pregnant 5 years ago, in 2005-6. At that time I had no knowledge of this MILAB scenario at all. I did not know what was going on because the UFO-researchers in Scandinavia neglect this subject and there is no open discussion about this military involvement at all in my country. We have only one New Age magazine, which promotes tarot-readers and lighthearted contactees and their supporters in UFO-community.

I just wondered about this sudden appearance of military and medical personnel during my abductions. The focal point of consciously realizing my MILAB connection was the precipitating incident, which "coincidentally" delayed my Multiple Sclerosis diagnosis 2 years ago. My diagnosis was not given in proper ways, because my qauda equina operation was initially delayed and there was a professional error made by a local doctor. The surgery left me with an untreated infection, which created a permanent inflammatory problem with the central nervous system. The unbelievable doctor's behavior caused a huge amount of mental stress and a short episode of dissociation, which affected the way my brains functioned. This actually caused me to remember things I should not have. I became conscious in a way the shadow government would not want me to be.

In hindsight, I realize many of these major events and turning points of my life are produced and controlled by aliens. And this is the most important factor I'm going to pinpoint out later.

*Why do you believe or have you been told by the aliens or military "handlers" why they are using you in their experiments? Are you a hybrid or genetically modified by aliens?*

The aliens have used me because I live in a genetically modified body. My physical existence offers an opportunity for the aliens to make genetic surveillance in a multigenerational way. When I say genetically modified, it is my understanding that this means an alteration of DNA so that the nervous system modified with alien DNA – and energetic body as well – can sustain the alien consciousness because only this kind of consciousness can make a hybrid body functional, per se. This is actually part of the soul recycling technology.

When I say I am a hybrid I understand myself – my consciousness is something you refer to as Draconian. I was obligated before birth to move into an altered body to fulfill my task. To perform that transition, I had to choose the human parents too, as long as the mother was a blood type RH negative factor. This immunological trait is a common feature among these so called Draconians and their reproduction.

But having an Rh-negative blood type doesn't mean you are a hybrid, it's just a necessary condition to carry on the biological technology. The genetic modification is very tied to CNS (central nervous system) functions and immunological moderation. This alien genetic factor includes modification of consciousness, a.k.a. vibrational aspects of soul/consciousness matrix as well. The soul matrix is a vibration, like electricity, in that it can be observed as tones of frequencies. The question of genetic alteration is not purely physical, as we understand. It includes vibrational factors as well.

My understanding of Draconian DNA is that it is basically inorganic, unlike the human DNA. The Draconian body-DNA function needs radiation to sustain consciousness like humans need air to breathe. The Draconian DNA structure is not a spiral alpha helix but a denser form of some inorganic and energetic matter, which could be described as a quadrangle. With this quadrangle the structures of energetic tones are organized to serve bodily functions. I believe this is why there have been procedures done to human DNA – balancing the functions and partitions of inorganic and organic matter within DNA. The fundamental building blocks for life are not quite what we have been told, apparently.

So, true hybrids have alien consciousness in an altered body via a genetic CNS modification. CNS modification is partly needed to handle the frequencies of alien consciousness with the energetic body. The alteration of CNS-genetics is done outside the womb during the impregnation by technology, which can hold and change the soul matrix via magnetic field. The modified embryo is then implanted inside the womb of the Rh negative female. The different kind of alien soul matrix revives the function of the hybrid body and altered CNS function. (All hybrids are psychic).

So you may understand why the real hybrids are keeping the secret and silence. The various produced beings, through hybrid bodies, are altered outside the womb during the embryonic stage for other things as well, such as functioning in a different kind of environment, and they have higher tolerance for radiation as well. The radiation itself is not poison to some ET races at all. *[EL-This was shared with me BEFORE the Japanese nuclear incident on 3/11/011 at Fukishima.]*

I have been used as an incubator for alien hybrid embryos.

The Rh negative factor is the key here. Many women abductees used in this way have the Rh negative factor in their blood. The Rh negative factor prevents the possible autoimmune reaction during the early stages of alien pregnancy.

"Normal" females are also producing human embryos for aliens. These embryos are partly grown and used as a biological protein source for reptoids. Abducted humans – abductees – do not need genetic alteration if they are used for other biotechnological uses and consumption – for reptoids. So frankly put, as food. These reptile beings are able to grow large amounts of biologically "alive" tissue. This tissue can be cloned to make manufactured grey beings as well. This kind of tissue cannot be cloned forever without degeneration. That's why the aliens are abducting so many humans. All of us have to satisfy the need of food for a large alien civilization. It's so simple. We are not on the top of the food chain. This is something we just have admit to ourselves.

Many abductees tell us about the baby presentations made by the aliens. The whole thing – in my opinion– is just meant to do some psychological bonding to prevent resistance of human beings. Nothing more. The babies are presented, as more mature babies are probably human-alien hybrids made to use as servants later on.

My son is being abducted as well. He is genetically modified too. His birth was a miracle. We had to use ICSI-method (in vitro fertilization) in order to have a vibrant embryo to be placed. During my pregnancy in alien encounters, I was introduced to my son two times. The body was small, his skin pale. He had huge blue eyes and only a small amount of hair. When he came to see me with this "Nordic" looking figure, his consciousness was maintained in a classic hybrid-like body. And just like mine, his awareness joined the genetically altered human body during my delivery. He has described that kind of memory to me. We have an ultra strong connection, and we communicate also by using pure feelings.

Military want all the "cookies" I can give them – my genetics, my psychic abilities, and there is medical research being done that offers benefits for both involved parties and their co-operation as well. And they have plugged my son in to their operations as well. This was the main reason I decided to share my story: to tell people to wake up and fight for their freedom. We have to understand that there are multiple participants with multiple agendas related to abductions/MILAB activity. And more and more, I believe, the two – medical shadow groups and military are linking together.

It seems to me that human participants have to work for these alien beings in ever deeper levels than was previously imagined. This is one reason why I believe there is not going to be an open disclosure about the true nature of the alien encounters. Some human factions are too deep into this mess. The disclosure would risk the economical/scientific benefits and power these groups have gained via alien connection and cooperation.

When a human is abducted for a first time, s/he is being implanted. The military has the needed technology to track the signals emitted by the implants of these new abductees. The implants insert themselves within the central nervous system, when the connection is made; there is a signal, which the military can pick up. So, all the alien abducted people are possible MILAB victims – hence – ReAbs, if they posses something that can be beneficial to the military. No one is safe and the MK ultra days are not over. The military/shadow government has the identity of every single abductee in this world.

*What kinds of medical issues have you experienced that you believe to be due to abductions? Have you been mind controlled by them, how?*

Aliens have done several physical procedures. They have

taken bone marrow from my neck and hip with a long needle. They have collected ovum. They have put an implant into my nostril. They have collected tissue samples from my arm and knee.

Psychologically they have erased my memories and installed fake ones. They have used what felt like electrical vibrations straight into my frontal lobe to do mind control. One morning I found a puncture mark in the middle my forehead, after having strong feelings to not look in the mirror (suggestions by them to not look into the mirror), and when I saw the mark, I remembered how they put some kind of electric vibration into my brain somehow through that needle and I was told not to remember and not to talk.

And then they forced me to look at images of the dolphins again from a screen-like device. I see the dolphins every time when my subconscious is trying to bring something to the surface. They have caused pure emotional horror and enjoyed the ride. *[EL – I have nothing against dolphins and friendly higher intelligent species, it's just their image is being projected in screen memories to pacify our minds into complicity.]*

I have an autoimmune inflammation in my CNS, because the inflammation of peripheral nerves went straight to the CNS (following a surgery). The diagnosis is G 37.9, and still waiting to be confirmed as MS, the primary progressive form. The whole episode – with the delay of the operation and the inflammation going straight to the CNS – was, I believe, alien orchestrated and my body is now being used as a guinea pig for medical pharmaceutical research done by some faction of the military/shadow government. Because my body is altered, I have degeneration in my pelvic and cervical area as well.

I have had a neuropsychological evaluation twice. I'm suffering from memory problems and visual-spatial problems, as well. The findings refer to an organic nature of impairment. I cannot work because of my physical and neuropsychological condition. Some of these changes can be explained via MS, and some because of the mind control and the methods aliens and military use. There is no cure for this. I have been recommended for neuropsychological rehabilitation.

I have been told by Draconians that my body is genetically altered. My blood pressure is quite low and my average body temperature is somewhere between 35-35.5 degrees of Celsius. [37C = 98.6F, so it's between 95.0- 96.8 F]. My psychic abilities are far higher than average. I sense human emotions and thought forms as soon as I see a person. This is something I would like to get rid of, because it wears me out. I prefer solitude and vibrationally developed, disciplined emotions like gratitude, etc. Unfortunately, there are not so many people possessing these features. I believe I have also been used to test Draconian weaponry modified for human military use because of my psychic abilities and vibrations. Some weapons can only be activated through psychic influence.

*Have you recognized any of the locations you have seen in your milab/abduction experiences such as DUMBS (Deep Underground Military Bases) or medical facilities? Have you recognized any human personnel you have seen in your "regular life" accidentally?*

I have been in a DUMB several times that I can consciously remember. One place I believe – merely my own speculation – is located somewhere in Canada or in the northern part of USA. The speculation is based only on visual observation of the nature. When I got out from underground I saw these huge trees I have seen on nature documentaries in my country. It was a mountain area, in the middle of the forest. And there was a railway entering in to the DUMB. The entrance was open and there was fence around the yard.

The other place was a nuclear silo, in a place were nuclear weapons were stored. These places could be one and the same, but somehow I doubt that.

I have seen the same medical personnel who treated me at the university hospital Department of Neurology, during the process of my neurological diagnosis. There is one professor of clinical neuroimmunology and neurophysiology and one medical doctor of neurology who are using me in their medical research done for the shadow government.

This medical research is dealing with the use of nitro-oxide as a regulator in the immune response of the CNS. Nitro-oxide is under constant interest in pharmaceutical work. (Not to be confused with dental nitrous oxide) Applications can be used in cardiovascular and pulmonary diseases and in asthma, as well. There are experiments made to use the asthma medication to relieve the symptoms of MS flares. So, the connection between my condition, these doctors, and MILAB abduction is to understand and regulate the immune response in the human nervous system.

I believe I'm under interest because of my genetic differences, too. So I'm serving multiple purposes which I probably even don't know about. One factor, in my opinion, is their interest in understanding how to connect together different types of neurological tissues without creating the usual degenerative autoimmune reaction. As one can understand, the application of this information is huge. One can do the digging by themselves by Googling nitro-oxide and CNS. It is all there.

The professor I saw in a DUMB is closely connected to a major pharmaceutical company. The same company is developing a drug for narcolepsy as well, and the nitro-oxide is playing an important role once again. I believe I'm used to test the narcotic influence of different medicines, as well. The medical researcher I'm talking about is doing research on the neurophysiological aspects of dreams, as well.

I also had one very important condition they needed in their study. I did not have plaques in my brain or spinal cord. These kinds of findings are implications of the primary progressive form of MS. All the people in my area suffering from this type of illness are being sent to these specific doctors for evaluation. Surprisingly. In this specific university hospital, there is a highly respected research group doing studies about the nitro-oxide finding as an indicator of brain atrophy in primary progressive MS. This specific university hospital and some personnel of this research group have been doing medical research and evaluation for the military people too. So there is a huge network going on, not only nationally but globally too. And the unfortunate ones (MILABs) are being plugged in.

Nitro-oxide NO is under constant interest in pharmaceutical work. In 1998 doctors Furchgott, Ignarro, and Murad were given a Nobel Prize for their research work related to NO.*

Nitric oxide plays a role in immune response as well and there is constant research being done on this subject.** The applications for NO are drugs developed and under development for neurological diseases as well, like Frampidrine for walking difficulties and muscle weakness for people suffering neurological diseases.***

Before this accident I was not interested in pharmacology in any level. I only had one conscious memory of the nurse who came to me when I was sitting on the research table, in a DUMB probably. She had a needle and she injected some liquid in to my right knee. "This is nitrixide" (that's what I first remembered), she said. "You should not make such a fuss about things." After that, I saw the same medical researcher entering the room. That's all I remember. And all I needed to remember to start to do my own checking out. I have taken photos from my knees after the nitro-oxide shots as well.

---

* http://nobelprize.org/nobel_prizes/medicine/laureate s/1998/press.html

** http://www.asahi-net.or.jp/~jr9h-szk/juku/juku3.pdf

*** http://www.chemicalbook.com/ChemicalProductProperty_EN_CB9853687.htm

So, it's no wonder these events were manipulated to the point where the delayed operation caused an autoimmune response in my CNS. I was a good catch. And this is only the tip of the iceberg from the work of this hidden network. I'm sure of it. But to go deeper into this could be a story of its own.

*What kinds of aliens are primarily working on your case? Can you describe their basic jobs and goals?*

Primarily reptoids, greys, and other aliens like mantis-creatures, because they are working under Draconian control. Before I continue, I have to clarify the position of reptiles and Draconians in order to understand what is going on and by whom.

Dracionians do not conduct abductions per se as the interdimensional reptiles are doing, even though they are occasionally seen in the UFO. Dracionians control the reptilian race and their behavior and the reptiles are servants for the Draconians. Draconians need the hybrid bodies to be used as containers for consciousness, because only a vibrant soul-matrix can reinforce manufactured hybrid bodies. There are a lot of species co-working in these scenarios, so it's difficult to define what kind of role the different ET creatures are playing from our point of view. Positive, neutral, or negative.

When I generally speak about hybrids, I don't know whether they are human-reptilian, human-Draconian, or human-some other race/races. And the other abductees and UFO-researchers don't know that for sure either. So pinpointing hybrids only as a reptilian human origin, we can do crucial damage for the hybrid rhetoric as a whole.

Reptoids are servants for the Draconian race. There are not so many Dracos on Earth, physically present. I have seen them only working in this particular nuclear silo. Reptoids are allowed to use humans as a resource and do their thing as long as they don't disobey the Draconian administration. By using hybrids, Draconians can produce workers, biological material etc., (who knows) for their use. Reptilians do the needed work. They abduct people and hybrids for the use of cloning and further production. They have advanced technological development to do that and they are allowed to use humans for their own purposes as well, primarily for nutrition and entertainment. By entertainment I mean sexual activities with humans. These sexual behaviors have malevolent, sadomasochistic features.

In other words, there is a vast biological industrial activity going on where humans are being used as a source for biological and psychological-emotional material. The basic job for reptoid-beings is to survive and carry their own cultural-genetic traits. This is something we have to understand. They do what they do because they are what they are – highly intelligent beings capable of remarkable things.

We have to step out of the victimized state of mind and get rid of the fear. This is the only way to get the respect of these creatures and develop a communication of some sort. Whining and unnecessary complaining are the dead end, then we start to dig our own psychological and physical grave for sure. Objectivity and courage is needed even to try to understand a different kind of intelligence and technology. This is something we are not able to do. The researchers who only feed the fear instead of objectivity are no better than the New Age people who are proclaiming easy ascension and waiting for spiritual enlightenment – even while being roasted in the oven.

I believe these reptoid creatures are the main problems and bullies for humans. And these reptoids do shapeshift and can take the form of these so-called Nordics as well. Draconians are far more advanced than humans are capable of even understanding. I have consciously seen dark brown Draconians with wings and hoofs. They are a highly technically advanced, warrior-like race with great disciplined actions. Draconians are also philosophical creatures and can be very fearless if needed. Females are superior to male. They consider themselves to be more sophisticated than humans. Because they are ranked quite high in hierarchy of different races, we rarely see them like we see the most highly ranked bosses in our companies. They mingle with their own kind of company.

I remember being in a silo barefoot and this male Draconian came to me and sent me a mental thought that he finds the human feet very big and repulsive. I found it funny, because during that episode I could not even understand where I was. Their goal is to continue their lives as a race as well. Just like we humans do.

It is odd but very often, in the MILAB ops scenarios we are not allowed to wear shoes, and our clothes may be lying in one place, later to be put on, but we never have our shoes. It's like we are not allowed to wear them. In my opinion there are couple of reasons why MILABs remember being without their shoes or clothes. One reason is the fact, that some MILABs are involved with research for example, related to radiation and they are being decontaminated after testing. This can partly explain the memories of showers and locker rooms. The other reasons why some MILABs are not wearing shoes are the satanic rituals, performed in DUMB, and their participation in these rituals under mind control. Being without shoes is serving ritual necessities and psychological manipulation, as well. Remember the Nazi concentration camps?

Reptoids are divided into interdimensional beings and some creatures that live under the surface of Earth. These creatures live in caverns and have red eyes and dark brown skin. They eat meat, too. Interdimensional reptoids can shapeshift and are predator-natured.

I have observed a conflict between the Draconians and some reptoid party/faction. It's about power. There was a military faction assisting – willingly or unwillingly, I'm not sure – and these specific reptoid groups are trying to overcome the Draconian leadership, because the Draconians are in charge of some nuclear military DUMBS, too. If this reptoid rebellion is proceeding, I'm feeling worried because this would mean the total loss of control made by Draconians. Reptoids would be allowed to mess around and even the shadow government would not be safe. If considering this as a chess game, the situation is not pleasant from the human point of view. But this is merely my speculation.

I saw the power struggle personally during an abduction. The Draconian entity came to stop the reptoids and prevented them from using me somehow. This has happened two times. So I guess I have something to offer to these Draconians and shadow government, and that's why they keep an eye on me.

The reptoids have expressed very violent activities towards me and some other abductees I have seen on the UFO, like beating, etc. I believe they are having a hard time trying to suppress their basic need to kill. And that's why some abductees are reporting very disturbing violent abductions and treatment.

The degeneration of personality traits and grappling for power applies to other species as well. By this degeneration I mean the need to produce unnecessary suffering while enjoying it.

There is also an original Grey race, per se. They are workers for these reptilian entities. And there are a huge amount of manufactured grey look-alike beings used for physical labor. They are being manufactured inside a DUMB and some are being transported to other locations.

*Many MILABs and now the popularized "supersoldiers" have described being used as operatives under mind control physically across the globe and even off world. They also describe virtual reality experiences, a term popularized by the late Dr. Karla Turner. Can you tell me if you can tell the difference between a true physical abduction, and one that is virtual reality?*

Yes. But this is only my experience. In my case true physical abductions leave marks. Something is done to my physical body. Sometimes there can be menstrual irregularities and abdominal pain, bruises, needle marks, scars, etc. The consciousness is totally controlled during these episodes. I can remember flashes of 1-10 seconds. Then I remember being shut down. My field of observation is narrowed. I can sometimes see clearly tiny areas at one time, like clear small windows of clarity in a limited field of vision. Sometimes I can feel being moved and pushed, even when I'm unable to open my eyes or when I'm in a dream-like state. In physical abductions, I get more of a drugged feeling and less clear memory, and lots of blank spots in-between. Most of the time these memories – whether physical or virtual reality – are very hard to separate because of the consciousness control.

Nowadays military don't walk into your house anymore. Trust me. They can open a time/space portal and pick you up so that you don't even notice.

The main objective for these aliens is not to be noticed. They prefer to stay in the shadows, because otherwise humans could start to do preventative actions to stop the abductions by strengthening their lucidity, using and developing proper technology for resistance. So we are not dealing with gods. We are dealing with mortal entities.

In the virtual reality experiences, it is as real as watching a movie or living an everyday life, with no observable limitations. With lucidity, realizing you are dreaming you can wake up from this scenario. In VRE, there is always some aspect of "strangeness" involved if one is able to recognize this. By this I mean for an example, a different kind of phone you have never seen before, strangers, furniture, etc. By recognizing these, you can achieve lucidity and wake up in your bed. But this is hard, because the VRE is produced in your brains by using methods like signals and electrical stimulation, which affects your neural and muscular function as well. This makes the scenario seem even more real. And physical/mental adjustment is being done under VRE situations. This makes the scenario seem even more real. By this I mean psychological conditioning on how to act or control oneself during RV-operations, behavioral modification on how to handle fear, tolerate pain, etc. True physiological modification, implanting, is being done either in a DUMB or in a UFO.

Reptoids use VRE for harvesting emotions too. This happens by causing horrifying VRE experiences for abductees. The military and aliens as well can produce VRE by sending signals to implants. Military can change these induced brainwaves into images and sounds on a screen. Aliens don't need that kind of technology, because they sense these telepathically.

I have been able to observe the exact moment when I'm being activated for the use. This happens when I'm going to sleep. Just when my brainwaves are starting to change for a sleep mode, I see a flash of bright light in my "minds" eye, even with eyes shut. Usually the scene "in my eyes" changes, and I get an impression of an open space in front of my closed eyes. I can also see from what kind of interior I'm been plugged into.

So there is a radar-like computer network through which abductees can be controlled. There is also portable equipment that have antenna, which can send the VRE signals, too. And some factions of the perpetrators are using this for their own purposes. I believe the connection can function in two ways: Once the abductee is able to use heightened psychic capacity and lucidity, one can attain information from the other party by doing remote viewing. I have been able to this once and then I saw the warehouse from where the signal was sent.

One has to understand that we are dealing with high technology, which most people don't know – even the moderate applications can be seen in a use in everyday life. For example, one "official" branch of this technology is being introduced to people as different kinds of computer related appliances for handicapped people. One can do their own research on this subject if interested.

*Have you ever been tasked by your MILAB controllers to do remote viewing? If so, how is this experience compared to the entrained "VRE" scenarios?*

Yes I have. I have been sent to observe some alien creatures (Draconian related) several times. I have also been used for more mundane issues, like checking some locks or paper documents. These were written in English — that I could remember. Remote viewing is produced either by physical abuse (and splitting of consciousness) or by using the VRE related technology. Consciousness can be separated and moved by using some sort of electrical vibration.

I can tell the difference between the RV and VRE by observing the visual scene I'm seeing. In RV, my vision is somehow truly controlled. It feels to me like I'm watching the environment through a bottle. The vision is somehow twisted and distorted. I see only the things I'm told to observe. I can do some conscious reasoning during these episodes as well. Sometimes there can be unwanted reaction and the RV situation is slipping into a spontaneous out-of-the-body experience. When this happens, I hear a buzzing sound in my ears and I have problems controlling the movements of my energy body. I can slip through the walls recklessly until I'm being drawn back to my body. Also, in RV there is seldom any physical sensation, pain, etc., present. Naturally. So only by lucidity and deep reflection one can discern these different kinds of phenomena. Very often remote viewing and virtual reality they are also linked together.

*What do you think is going on with the hybrid issue as popularized by Dr. David Jacobs in his alien abduction case histories? Have you seen alien-human hybrids in your experi-*

*ences? What do you believe is their real function?*

When we are talking about the hybrid-issue, we have to understand that as a human race we don't really have the complete picture of this issue. There are not as many genetically different alien related hybrids on earth as some researchers are stating. That's for sure. To say alien hybrids are all malevolent, suffering from severe personal disorders is as narrow-minded approach as New Agers have, when saying that alien agenda is good and hybrids are a way to save humankind. Nonsense.

Based on what I have experienced, true alien hybrids are here to serve the surveillance of the genetic study made by the alien race. Hybrids are not to meant to infiltrate into human society to fulfill some hidden purposes of Draconians or reptiles. This is something one has to understand. Hybrids are used just to produce more hybrids for the use of Draconians. Hybrids are used like machines in Draconian bioindustry. We have no knowledge why this alteration is being made. Our social or emotional life per se is not under interest of any kind. Hybrids of the more alien types I mentioned live their lives in different societies like other people do.

When I speak about hybrids, I consider them to be Draconian/alien consciousnesses in an altered human body. But I'm sure that reptoids have their own breeding program going on which is something Draconians consider not suitable behavior – rebellion. So yes, there are reptilian hybrids – reptilian consciousnesses in human altered bodies. And then there are genetic mixtures of many other races as well, made by Dracos which are not connected to human race at all.

According to my understanding and memories, we cannot define a hybrid just by observing the differences of the DNA structures between hybrids and humans, because some of the changes are energetic in nature, as I said before.

The major difference is the heightened psychic ability

compared to other human beings. When I say I consider myself to be alien-hybrid, aka a genetically modified human with alien soul matrix consciousness, I know there should be a genealogist to confirm my statement to make this official proof. It is not even important to me, because I have to live an ordinary everyday life, anyway (and of course deal with the constant interference in my life.) I do not see myself mean or malevolent in any way. Neither is my son. But people who are acting like judges, I consider to be dangerous. There is no room for hypocrisy.

Humans manipulate, torture, neglect and abuse their kind in similar ways that these reptoids are doing to achieve their own agenda. Wake up time. Instead of this, we should concentrate on real issues, which are the alien manipulation through their hive-like almost organic influence, and the possessions they can take over certain individuals. These things have nothing to with hybrids per se, like the ones I've defined. There can also be observed people with low vibrations and lack of integrity acting and playing with abductees. This has nothing to do with hybrids as well and the hybrid issue is something I consider to be less important in the field of abduction research. Wrong conclusions only create unnecessary fear.

Only by seeing the overall impact of this alien manipulation we can start to live our own lives in a more compassionate way. We need to find the true humanity of our own kind and not be willing to be an amusement for them to give them the vibes, or emotional reactions, that the reptoids like.

Another thing we have to wake up to understand is that the alien modification with hybrids (aka genetically modified human abductees) starts before physical manifestation, such as *in vitro* before birth, or while in the womb, and is carried on constantly in hybrid's lives. This means one can observe certain patterns in hybrids and abductees.

1. The abductors are creating an environment where the hybrid and/or abductee is often emotionally and socially

isolated either geographically or by parents. This provides them convenient ground to influence the life patterns of the hybrid and repress possible interference made by other human beings. Experimental control.

2. They often set up a love affair to mate the hybrid or abductee with a suitable candidate. Through this selected person, aliens can control the action of a hybrid (aka genetically modified human-abductee). This usually means that true hybrids are being kept "hidden" by preventing them from having a major position in modern society. This can be made by disrupting and orchestrating their education, relationships, and health, as was done in my case. So as one can understand, there is no glory to be had in this hybrid issue. There is only suffering if these patterns are not revealed and worked through, so as to gain personal and social integration of a hybrid person. (Secrecy and isolation harms us.)

Many of these aspects apply to abductees as well and can be produced by the shadow military government people, too.

I have seen so-called "hybrids" (the more alien ones only seen or existing on ships, etc.) during my abductions. They were merely showing me where to go, etc. I had no conversation with them that I could consciously remember. These beings were very short and gave me an impression of physical density of some sort. In the room I saw one of them was having modified air pressure given to them. I could imagine one can experience this by diving deep. I have also seen small horse looking, white creatures. They were kept in containers. And the hybrids are working to collect liquid from the ligaments of these creatures.

In order to understand the modern hybrid discussion, we need to accept the fact that most information is given by the abductees who are merely reporting the facts aliens want and allow them to see and "remember". And certain researchers are adding water to the mill by taking these fragment memories to form a theory. This, in my opinion is how the distortion is made and facts are neglected. We simply don't know what kind of genetic experiments are being done and by whom.

*Have you observed the alien possession of a human situation, such as the term "reptilian hosting" being used?*

Yes I have. I did not know the name for this subject until recently. Before going deeper into this issue I have to tell that Eve Lorgen has gone straight in to the heart of this alien discussion. Really. She has openly formed a view of alien manipulation, which I find to be true in my life. After I realized that, I was able to form some kind of synthesis made from my life. I did not know the idea or concept of Alien Love Bite until recently, but these three little words changed my life and showed me the way to self realization and more awareness to fight for autonomy in my life.

Alien hosting does happen.

Regardless of that, I always subconsciously knew this kind of phenomenon was happening in my life. By hosting, I refer to a person who is under direct influence of a reptoid being, mainly through mind control. Sometimes the reptile's spirit can enter a person's body and cause some changes in the physical appearance of the hosted person, as well. Facial features can change, their voice, etc. These changes can be seen and often are observed even consciously. But mostly they are neglected because the other partner or persons close to them don't understand what is going on. I believe many hosted people are considered to suffer from psychiatric diseases like personality disorders, *[EL – like narcissistic, sociopathic]* psychotic behavior even the problems have different etiology than in normal F-code (DSM) diagnosis. In my opinion, the hosting occurs within the orchestrated relationships.

It is done if there is a need from the reptiles to cause immediate influence on the hybrid's/abductee's life during certain periods of time, like to have the other partner feeling emotions such as fear and abandonment. Possession occurs when the reptilian being itself wants to experience directly emotions and physical stimulus through a hybrid's/abductee's body. *[EL – it can occur with non-abductees too.]*

The other term closely connected to hosting is the reptilian hive-mind. The term hive-mind in my understanding is the needed reptilian matrix or created context in hybrid's lives. By this I mean that the reptiles are capable of creating a reality matrix, like a Nintendo game. Reality matrix contains certain amount of freedom for abductee or hybrid to make decisions in their life, but nevertheless the outcome is what the reptiles want it to be. By using this hive mind manipulation, many people can be included in the matrix to act as wanted for the needed result.

The reptilian hive-mind is being activated as a lure like episode often among multiple needed participants to create the needed situations into hybrids or abductees lives. This has happened to me many times in my life and during these situations I felt quite powerless to change the course of the events I could already know was going to happen.

The Hive mind, or created reality matrix, is usually deactivated once the needed result is gained. For example, marriage – in my case – and the delayed surgery and so on. *[EL – This can extend to sabotaged media efforts to have guests on to tell their stories, where certain aspects of the alien agenda are never allowed to be spoken in a large way in the public domain.]*

After the deactivation of the "hive mind" the people involved often seem to wake up somehow. They may feel shame about what they have done and don't seem to understand how they could not have seen the results of their behavior. In this way the reptilians can enjoy the caused misery two times, once with hybrid or abductee and secondly with the other manipulated participants. *[EL – Who, by the way, are non-abductees and ARE VERY MUCH AFFECTED BY THIS TOO – and are less aware than the abductees themselves are.]*

I could tell you examples of people who are under hosting or shape shifting reptiles per se in my opinion, but I'd rather not. If I would start to pinpoint people, I would not act any better than people who infer all the hybrids are one bunch of sociopathic monsters. Instead I would encourage people to judge others based on their actions, like Jesus was doing. Actions reveal the color of one's heart. Not the words or appearance.

My husband was under reptilian hosting and hive-mind influence when we met almost 20 years ago. Without going into specific details, the pattern was clearly seen. He was compulsive, neglectful, aggressive, and he constantly created disturbance in my life during the key points in my life I considered that were critical for my work. I did lot of work with confronting him to pull him out of the lure. The lure – being the reptilian hive mind that was trying to control his behavior and thoughts. And I did a good job. Today, I have great husband and we work as a team.

In the early years of our relationship, he was an abductee, too. There were also very intense times of paranormal activity, too. I'm quite aware that aliens and the shadow government people manipulate him on regular basis. By this I mean that subconsciously he is monitoring my behavior. *[EL – aka a handler as a sleeper agent.]* Even while writing this, he is quite restless. He cannot concentrate to anything, etc. But the situation is under control, because I know what is going on. And he has begun to recognize his own behavior, too. I can sense he is worried because he is aware of my disclosure and the spooky calls, and that at the same time he is under the command too. Not easy part to play for him.

Now I'm being played off the field by the reptiles and the hive-mind synchronized events. I live in the middle of the forest on a pension disability. I cannot move long distances and my memory is playing tricks on me. They did a great job!

Also, at the same time, I can sense a relief. I feel something is moving away from my life. And I begin to see life differently, being more present. The reptilians and shadow government have changed their tactics. After such a long period of negativity, good "accidents" have started happen. I'm holding my breath. I know these synchronized events are manipulated as the previous years of my life, but I can handle that by not being emotionally too attached with these events. Even though I know I cannot ever really be free from this mess, there is a pause from negative tactics and I have waited for that. So this whole thing means that "we" are having negotiations of my limited freedom. I'm being given threats on my life in VRE and at the same time I'm being given candies as well.

As one can understand, the issue of alien manipulated relationships and events are, in my opinion, much more important than an isolated study of abduction experiences. Only by seeing a bigger alien picture can we understand the overall impact aliens have in our lives. They own us. They control us. And this happens in ordinary relationships all over the world. *[EL – This is what Barbara Bartholic and myself have believed for years.]*

*Have you ever seen or observed the human clones in your experiences?*

Yes I have. In a DUMB I have seen my clone. Somehow it was not properly made. The tissues looked puffy. This creature could barely walk and it was wobbling. Movements were very clumsy and the scenario reminded me of the Frankenstein's story. Somehow I believe human participants made this clone.

In UFO craft I have consciously seen male clones, lots of them, lying on the tables. I saw this accidentally when a hybrid creature was showing me the way to somewhere. I think this was not meant for my eyes to observe, but accidents do happen.

I strongly believe that, almost 13 years ago, my original body was killed and used somehow. My consciousness was put into cloned body. *[EL – This happened to Ted Rice and was elaborated on in the late Dr. Karla Turner's Masquerade of Angels book.]* At that time, I felt physically different and looked younger. My friend also told me that I looked different. But I have no conscious memories of this. Only my instinct. The procedure was conducted after very sadomasochistic events by the reptoids and humans, which I do not want to go into specific detail. But the process of soul recycling (after being born into a body) begins after abductees are given some sort of liquid to drink. I had to drink it, as well, as a couple I had not seen before. What happened to them, I don't know. I also experienced being killed (in a ritualized fashion) a second time in the autumn of 2010, similar procedure and I have conscious memories of that incident.

I was spontaneously awakened in the 2010 "storage in a black box" procedure, where the pure consciousness, essence of me was temporarily kept. I know these issues are frightening and sound psychotic. Only a very strong person is able to go deeply into these disturbing experiences without being shocked. The denial of these soul-recycling procedures is natural for humans and I can understand that clearly. I'm telling this because the facts and witness testimonies cannot be ignored forever. Behind the surface there are more things happening than friendly discussions with the space brothers.

I can give you one thought to contemplate: What the term karma is given to people as a justifier for their memories of previous lives, which they lived because their consciousnesses had been recycled by the aliens may not be because of the karmic law. In my opinion we don't know what is the natural process of consciousness to transform or move forward. We only know that we have been told to behave or otherwise we could wake up as pigs. We are being told that we remember past lives because of reincarnation, not because someone has reincarnated us. There is a huge difference here and I believe the technology for doing this is being kept hidden and it would be very precious for humanity if they don't already have it.

# Suggested Reading

Behary, Wendy. *Disarming the Narcissist: Surviving & Thriving with the Self-Absorbed.* Oakland, CA: New Harbinger Publications, Inc., 2008

Bernstein, Albert J. *Emotional Vampires: Dealing with People Who Drain You Dry.* New York, NY: McGraw Hill, 2001

Brown, Sandra. *How To Spot a Dangerous Man Before You Get Involved.* Berkekey, CA: Hunter House Inc., 2005

Bruce, Robert. *The Practical Psychic Self-Defense Handbook: A Survival Guide.* Charlottesville, VA: Hampton Roads Publishing, Company, 2011

Dale, Cyndi. *Energetic Boundaries; How to Stay Protected and Connected in Work, Love and Life.* Boulder, CO: Sounds True, 2011

Glass, Lillian. *Toxic Men: Ten Ways to Identify, Deal with and Heal from the Men Who Make Your Life Miserable.* Avon, MA: Adams Media, 2010

Mahoney, Willliam, K. *Exquisite Love: Heart-Centered Reflections on the Narada Bhakti Sutra.* The Woodlands, TX: Anusara Press, 2010

Peck, Scott M. *People of the Lie.* New York, NY: Simon & Schuster Inc., 1983

## Bibliography

Belanger, Michelle. *The Psychic Vampire Codex: A Manual of Magick and Energy Work.* San Francisco, CA: Weiser Books, 2004

Dixon, J.M. *The Weiser Field Guide to Vampires: Legends, Practices, and Encounters Old and New.* San Francisco, CA: Weiser Books, 2009

Ford, Arielle. *Hot Chocolate for the Mystical Lover.* New York, NY: Plume, 2001

Joudry P. & Pressman, M. *Twin Souls: Finding your True Spiritual Partner.* Center City, MN: Hazelden, 1995

Katherine, Anne. *Boundaries: Where You End and I Begin.*

New York, NY: Simon & Schuster, 1991

Lorgen, Eve. *The Love Bite: Alien Interference in Human Love Relationships*. Bonsall, CA: ELogos & HHC Press, 2000

Rosenberg, Marshall. *Nonviolent Communication: A Language of Life*. Encinitas, CA: Puddle Dancer Press, 2005

Rogers, S. *Mindsweep: Advanced Technology, The Alien Agenda and The Afterlife*. Merrimack, NJ: Write to Print, 2003

Slate, Joe. *Psychic Vampires: Protection from Energy Predators and Parasites*. St. Paul, MN: Llewellyn Publications, 2002

Swann, Ingo. *Psychic Sexuality: The Bio-Psychic Anatomy of Sexual Energies*. Rapid City, South Dakota: Ingo Swann Books, 1999

## Online Source URLs

Bigelow Roper Poll Information: http://www.viewzone.com/abduct.htm

Compassionate Communication: Jerry Donoghue, http://www.ashevilleccc.com

Cupid: http://cupid.askdefine.com/ , http://www.crystalinks.com/cupid.html

Emotional Intelligence: http://www.unh.edu/emotional_intelligence/ei%20What%20is%20EI/ei%20definition.htm http://www.ihhp.com/what_is_eq.htm

Dr. Corrado Malanga and Flash Mental Simulation Procedure (FMS): http://flashmentalsimulation.wordpress.com/corradomalanga/

Paranormal Survey Statistics: http://en.wikipedia.org/wiki/Paranormal

Professionals in the Helping Industries and Their Personal Pathological Relationships: http://saferelationshipsmagazine.com/professionals-in-the-helping-industries-and-their-personal-pathological-relationships-2 and http://saferelationshipsmagazine.com/

about/what-we-believe

Psychic Vampirism Youtube Video Clip: http://www.youtube.com/watch?v=Sz9cEjNFOvs

Excerpts taken for Wiz and Koral Story: "The Vipers Enchantment" by Wiz Kinnigin http://www.kininigin.com/VIPER%20STORY%20I.htm

## About the Author:

**Eve Lorgen**, MA, has over 20 years experience consulting individuals with anomalous trauma and the paranormal. Her warm, compassionate style of communication and unique expertise has helped people all over the globe understand and receive support regarding their anomalous trauma. In her early years of alien abduction research, she discovered that ordinary investigative and scientific methods alone could not adequately deal with the reality of otherworldly interference in human affairs. Our strength as humanity lies in the power of true love and a deep connection with our divine soul. Eve is now dedicated to helping others deepen their own soul connection, develop emotional intelligence and wisely discern in the matters of love. Originally from California, she now lives in the mountains of Western North Carolina, has an active consulting practice, enjoys yoga, meditation, gardening, and writing.

Printed in Poland
by Amazon Fulfillment
Poland Sp. z o.o., Wrocław